Baedeker's

BUDAPEST

Imprint

82 colour pictures, 7 plans, 7 ground-plans, 1 graphic representation, 1 transport plan, 1 city plan

Text: Helmut Linde, Reutlingen
Editorial work: Baedeker staff

General direction:
Dr Peter Baumgarten, Baedeker Stuttgart

Cartography: Georg Schiffner, Lahr
Franz Kaiser, Sidelfingen,
Cartographia, Budapest (city plan)

Source of illustrations:
Anthony (1), Handl (12), Historia-Photo (9), IBUSZ (14), IPV (17), Jenninger (1), Lammel (1), Linde (17), MDV (2), Oberländer (6)

English Translation: Alec Court/David Cocking

Reproductions:
Gölz Repro-Service GmbH, Ludwigsburg

Following the tradition established by Karl Baedeker in 1844, sights of particular interest and hotels of particular quality are distinguished by either one or two asterisks.

To make it easier to locate the various sights listed in the "A to Z" section of the Guide, their coordinates on the city plan are shown in red at the head of each entry.

Only a selection of hotels and restaurants can be given: no reflection is implied, therefore, on establishments not included.

In a time of rapid change it is difficult to ensure that all the information given is entirely accurate and up to date, and the possibility of error can never be entirely eliminated. Although the publishers can accept no responsibility for inaccuracies and omissions, they are always grateful for corrections and suggestions for improvement.

© Baedeker Stuttgart
Original German edition

© 1991 Jarrold and Sons Ltd
English language edition world-wide

© 1991 The Automobile Association
United Kingdom and Ireland

US and Canadian edition
Prentice Hall Press

Distributed in the United Kingdom by the Publishing Division of The Automobile Association, Fanum House, Basingstoke, Hampshire, RG21 2EA

Licensed user:
Mairs Geographischer Verlag GmbH Co.,
Ostfildern-Kemnat bei Stuttgart

Printed in Italy by G. Canale & C. S.p.A – Borgaro T.se – Turin

0–13–094723–7 US and Canada
0 7495 0280 0 UK

Contents

The Principal Sights at a Glance

Preface

This Pocket Guide to Budapest is one of the new generation of Baedeker guides.

Baedeker pocket guides, illustrated throughout in colour, are designed to meet the needs of the modern traveller. They are quick and easy to consult, with the principal sights described in alphabetical order and practical details about opening times, how to get there, etc., shown in the margin.

Each guide is divided into three parts. The first part gives a general account of the city, its history, population, culture and so on; in the second part the principal sights are described; and the third part contains a variety of practical information designed to help visitors to find their way about and make the most of their stay.

The new guides are abundantly illustrated and contain numbers of newly drawn plans. At the back of the book is a large city map, and each entry in the main part of the guide gives the coordinates of the square on the map in which the particular feature can be located. Users of this guide, therefore, will have no difficulty in finding what they want to see.

Facts and Figures

Arms of the
Hungarian Capital
Budapest

General

Budapest, the capital of the Hungarian People's Republic is considered by many visitors to be the "Paris of the East", because of its particular charm; after Moscow and Leningrad it is the most densely populated and economically and culturally the most important metropolis of Eastern Central Europe. Budapest came into being in 1872 by the amalgamation of three previously independent towns, Óbuda (Old Buda), Buda and Pest, and subsequently spread quickly on both sides of the Danube. Thanks to its favourable geographical position this leading political, administrative, industrial and commercial centre of Hungary maintains many different relations with important centres in Europe and elsewhere.

Metropolis

Budapest is the seat of the National Assembly (a single-chamber parliament) and all the important Government offices. Numerous universities, technical schools, museums, libraries and the Hungarian Academy of Science bear witness to the high status of its intellectual life, as do the many theatres and cultural institutions. Budapest is the meeting-place of several parliamentary committees of the Council for Economic Co-operation (RGW/COMECON). In addition, the Hungarian capital is the seat of the Danube Commission and the World Federation of Democratic Youth.

The richest thermal and mineral springs of Europe are to be found in the area of the city of Budapest. Some of the 123 springs have been used since Celtic times for therapeutic bathing purposes.

Spa

Budapest is in the Central Region of Hungary.

Region

Budapest is situated at 47° 29′ north and 19° 08′ east at a favourable spot for communication across the Danube, leading from Budai hegy-ség (the hills of Buda) on the threshold of the Hungarian Central Uplands, to the north-western edge of the Great Hungarian Plain (Alföld). The highest point of the city area is János-hegy (John's Hill); 529 m (1736 feet), situated in the hills of Buda to the west of the Danube. The lowest point of the city is in the region of Csepel-sziget (the island of Csepel) in the Danube at a height of 97 m (318 feet) above normal water-level.

Geographical Position

Topographical contrasts are a feature of the unique landscape. The territory of the city on the right of the Danube includes the river terraces of various heights and extends far into the Buda upland, which is composed of dolomite and chalk and which was articulated by a tectonic disturbance into a higher northern part (János-hegy, 529 m (1736 feet)) and a lower southern part (Gellért-hegy, 235 m (771 feet)). The plain of Pest on the left bank of the Danube is far more favourable to settlement, and has long been the focus of population of the Hungarian capital.

◀ *Council Building in Pest*

9

General

A special place is reserved for the three islands in the river: Obuda-sziget, Margit-sziget and Csepel-sziget.

Telephone Dialling Codes

From Great Britain: 010 361
From the USA and Canada: 011 361

Area

The city covers an area of 525 sq. km (203 sq. miles). About 173 sq. km (67 sq. miles) of the area of the city is on the right bank of the Danube and about 352 sq. km (106 sq. miles) on the left bank. Almost half of the city territory is built up; the remainder consists of open spaces (especially woods, areas of agricultural use and parks). The Hungarians are proud to call their capital the "greenest in Europe". The road network comprises 3700 km (2300 miles). Budapest extends from north to south approximately 25 km (16 miles) and from east to west about 29 km (18 miles).

City Districts

The area of the city is divided into twenty-one districts. On the right bank of the Danube:
Districts I, II, III, XI, XII, XXII
On the left bank of the Danube:
Districts IV, V, VI, VII, VIII, IX, X, XIV, XV, XVI, XVII, XVIII, XIX, XX
Danube Island Csepel:
District XXI
The commercial quarter of the Hungarian capital, which is not dissimilar to the central district of a Western city, is almost entirely within the area of District V (Pest's Danube bank). In little over 2·5 sq. km (1 sq. mile) there are concentrated not only numerous shops, businesses and boutiques which, with their wide range of articles, make Budapest now a leading shopping

Buda: view from Fishermen's Bastion over the Castle Palace to Gellért Hill

centre of eastern Europe, but here are also to be found Government administrative offices, financial and trade institutions as well as important cultural and scientific establishments. The density of population of District V is some 19,300 inhabitants per square kilometre (125,000 per sq. mile), with 38,000 workers per square kilometre (98,000 per sq. mile). More than 100,000 employees commute daily into District V. Districts I–III and VI–XIV form the central domiciliary and employment zones. More than 720,000 jobs are located here. The population density amounts to 3240 per square kilometre (1250 per sq. mile). Nearly half a million commuters arrive each day and another 470,000 leave to work elsewhere.

The fringe districts IV and XV–XXII comprise the outer domiciliary working districts. As well as modern estates there are large areas of houses with gardens, the majority of which are privately owned. More than half the 230,000 jobs which were set up here were created by modern industrial concerns.

Towards the end of the Second World War, Budapest suffered heavy destruction. In District I where German troops were holed up for a long time in the castle quarter, almost all the buildings were damaged or destroyed. After the end of the war rebuilding began, but suffered setbacks during the uprising in 1956. From 1960 to 1975 187,000 dwellings were either rebuilt or newly built. In recent years the reconstruction of architectural monuments has been enthusiastically pursued; especially spectacular at present are the plans to rebuild the castle quarter and the reconstruction of buildings in District V.

Rebuilding after the Second World War

Population and Religion

In 1720 the three independent towns of Óbuda, Buda and Pest had altogether 12,200 inhabitants. At that time the majority of the population lived in Buda. A hundred and ten years later the total population of the three towns had risen to 98,500 and the heaviest concentration had shifted to the Pest side of the river (60,500). When in 1873 the three towns were united to form Budapest, the combined population had already passed the 300,000 mark. After the successful accommodation with Austria in 1867 and the restoration of its position as the capital, Budapest experienced a remarkable upsurge which also resulted in a rapid growth of population. Shortly after the turn of the century a million people lived in Budapest; in the 1970s the 2-million mark was exceeded. In 1988 the Hungarian capital had 2,100,000 inhabitants, about 20 per cent of the population of the Hungarian People's Republic. Partly owing to changes in the birth rate and the drive to extend the regional lines of communication, the growth of population has recently slowed down considerably, and in addition another contrary development, which has occurred in other cities, has been the movement of people from the inner to the outer districts and to other suburbs of the conurbation. In District V alone, the population has declined between 1960 and today by some 16,000.

General

The largely self-governing Hungarian capital is regulated by law. The principal instrument of government is the city council, the members of which are elected every five years. Measures passed by the council are carried out by an executive committee which is led by a president (his position is similar to that of

Administration

an American state governor). A departmental head governs each specialist department.

Administration of the twenty-one city districts is the responsibility of a district council, the members of which are also elected for five years. The executive committees of the city district are led by chairmen (similar to mayors).

Religion

The majority of the citizens of Budapest who profess a religious belief are traditionally Roman Catholic (at present about 60 per cent). About a quarter are Protestants (the majority of them adherents of the Reformed Church), the others are spread among various religious groups (especially Orthodox and Baptist).

Minorities

By far the largest number of inhabitants of Budapest are of Magyar descent. Among minorities should be mentioned Gipsies and more especially Germans, Slovakians, Serbs, Croatians and Romanians.

Transport

Local traffic

Every year more than 1·6 million people use the local transport system of Budapest. They are among the most productive of their kind in the world.

HÉV

The surburban railway (HÉV) provides a fast link, with its four routes between the inner city and the smaller centres of Gödöllő, Csepel, Ráckeve and Szentendre on the periphery of the city.

Metro

The Underground (Metro) Railway at present has three lines: the first was opened as long ago as 1896, an east–west line came into operation in 1973 and a north-south line in 1979. The Underground system is to be extended.

Trams

The Budapest tramway system with its thirty-eight routes forms a very closely meshed network. The trams run at short intervals (on many routes there is a night service).

Bus

The most important local means of transport is the bus. In Budapest there are 208 bus and 12 trolley bus routes. A few lines are also in operation at night.

Other local transport

The rack railway up the Széchenyi-hegy, the chair-lift up the János-hegy, the funicular up Castle Hill, the Danube passenger ships and the minibus operating on Margaret Island have more the character of holiday and excursion transport.

Railway

Budapest is an important national and international railway junction. Rail traffic uses four large stations. Throughout the day international trains run between Budapest and all the important European cities. The most important international express trains are the EuroCity "Franz Lehár" (Vienna–Budapest), the EuroCity "Danube Courier" (Dortmund–Budapest), the "Orient Express" (Paris–Budapest), the "Viennese Waltzer" (Basle–Budapest) express and the "Metropol", "Hungaria" and Pannonia" express trains (all three Berlin–Dresden–Budapest).

Many trains at frequent intervals provide useful connections between Budapest and all the important places in Hungary.

Budapest's airport, Ferihegy I and II, 14 km (9 miles) south-east of the city centre, is the only international airport in the country. It is served by all the important east and west European airlines. The national airline Malév and its subsidiaries has services from here all over the world. While most travellers come from Western Europe, many also come from Tel Aviv, New York and Montreal.

Because of the rapid development in the numbers of both tourists and businessmen going to Hungary, the old Ferihegy I Terminal was bursting at the seams; the airport has recently been extended and modernised and Terminal II built. It can now handle 4 million passengers a year. Air freight within a year accounts for some 20,000 tonnes (three-quarters of which is freight leaving Budapest).

Airport

One of the largest ports on the Danube is on the west side of Csepel Island on the southern edge of the city. It has been developed into an international and national free port. In 1988 more than 3 million tonnes of freight was handled; 8 per cent of the entire import for the Hungarian capital was landed in Csepel. The most important goods in 1988 were building materials, fuel, mineral-oil products, ore, food and fodder.

Port

M0: Budapest motorway ring: length 90 km/56 miles (under construction)
M1 (E60/E75): Budapest–Györ (–Vienna–Bratislava)
M3 (E71): Budapest–Gyöngyös
M5 (E75): Budapest–Kecskemét
M7 (E71): Budapest–Siófok–Zamárdi
E77: Budapest–Vác–Parassapuszta (frontier)
E60: Budapest–Szolnok–Artánd (frontier)
E73: Budapest–Dunaújváros–Udvar (frontier)
E66: Budapest–Székesfehérvár–Veszprém (–Klagenfurt)
E77: Budapest–Debrecen
10: Budapest–Komárom–Györ
11: Budapest–Szentendre–Viségrad–Esztergom
30: Budapest–Gödöllő–Hatvan
70: Budapest–Erd–Székesfehérvár–Lepsény

Motorways, Europa Roads and important Main Roads

Culture

Budapest is the outstanding cultural centre of Hungary. The seat of the Hungarian Academy of Science, which developed from a successful foundation in 1825 by Count Széchenyi, is here; and most of the colleges and academies of the country are also concentrated in Budapest. Franz Liszt promoted the establishment of the Budapest Academy of Music, which today is world famous. More than two dozen theatres, outstandingly furnished museums and galleries are proof of the reputation of Budapest as a cultural city.

General

Magyar Tudományos Akadémia (Hungary Academy of Science, with ten departments: language and literature, philosophy and history, mathematics and physics, agriculture, medicine, technology, chemistry, biology, law and economics, mining and geology).
Allatorvostudományi Egyetem (Veterinary College). Budapesti Müszaki Egyetem (Technical University of Budapest).
Eötvös Loránd Tudományegyetem (Loránd Eötvös University;

Colleges and Academies

a successor to the university founded by Péter Pázmany in Tyrnau in 1635 and moved to Buda in 1777).

Kertészeti Egyetem (Horticultural University).

Marx Károly Közgazdaságtudományi Egyetem (Karl Marx University of National Economy).

Semmelweis Orvostudományi Egyetem (Semmelweis University of Medicine).

Allamigazgatási Főiskola (College of Administration).

Gyógypedagógiai Tanárképző Főiskola (College of Remedial Education).

Kereskedelmi és Vendéglátóipari Főiskola (College of Trade and Catering).

Külkereskedelmi Főiskola (College of External Trade).

Liszt Ferenc Zeneművészeti Főiskola (Franz Liszt Music Academy).

Magyar Iparművészeti Főiskola (College of Hungarian Arts and Crafts).

Magyar Képzőművészeti Főiskola (Hungarian College of Fine Art).

Magyar Testnevelési Főiskola (Hungarian College of Physical Education).

Orvostovábbképző Intézet (Further Education Institute of Medicine).

Pénzügyi és Számviteli Főiskola (College of Finance).

Szinház és Filmművészeti Főiskola (College of Drama and Cinematic Art).

Museums and Galleries

Budapest has four museums of international importance. The National Museum (archaeological and historical collection) provides a glimpse into the history of the country. In the Hungarian National Gallery, the Museum of Fine Arts and the Arts and Crafts Museum, masterpieces of Hungarian and European artists can be found. In addition the tourist will find informative exhibitions in the Museums of Ethnography, of Trade and Catering, Agriculture, Military History, the Workers' Movement, Natural Science and Literature, as well as in the Budapest Historical Museum and in over twenty other special collections.

Music and Theatre

Since the last century music has had an important place in Budapest, not least through the work of Franz Liszt. The names of the composers Béla Bartók, Zoltán Kodály and Sándor Szokolay, the conductors Janos Ferencsik, György Lehel and Jenő Ormandy, as well as the pianist György Cziffra (some of the artists named are today living abroad) are evidence of the standard of music in the cultural life of Budapest. The annual major events, the Budapest Spring Festival and Budapest Festival Weeks in the autumn, include important musical contributions. The Redoubt in Pest, the Erkel Theatre and auditoria of the Academy of Music, the Matthias Church, the Synagogue in Dohány Street, the Operetta Theatre and the new sports hall are the venues for a broad and diverse programme.

The Hungarian National Philharmonia, the Budapest Philharmonia, the Orchestra of Hungarian Radio and Television, the Budapest Madrigal Ensemble, the Franz Liszt Chamber Orchestra and the Budapest Chamber Ensemble, together with the Schola Hungarica are well known in musical circles outside Hungary.

With more than two dozen theatres, Budapest is among the leading theatrical cities of eastern Europe. Abroad, this reputation is especially represented by the Hungarian State Popular

Morning light on the Danube (Parliament Building)

Art Ensemble, which is devoted to the maintenance of cultural assets. The leading theatres are the National Theatre, the Erkel Theatre, the Madách Theatre, the Pest Theatre, the Pest Redoubt, the Castle Theatre, the Josephtown Theatre, the People's Theatre, the Attila-József Theatre, the University Theatre and the Theatre of Comedy. Ballet, dance and pantomime have a home in the new sports hall.

Trade and Industry

Budapest is one of the leading economic centres of the Warsaw Pact countries. It is the headquarters of several international economic organisations of socialist countries (including Agromasch, Intermetall, Intransmasch). Thanks to its opportunities for employment, the Hungarian capital attracts daily more than 250,000 commuters. Today in Budapest about 1·1 million people are employed, most of them in the industrial sector (over 40 per cent) and the service sector (40 per cent). A feature of the economic structure of the capital is the large proportion of high technological and export-oriented branches of industry (engineering and vehicle manufacture, chemistry, metallurgy, electro-technology and electronics, textiles).

General

A very favourable location, and hence communications, coal supplies in the vicinity and the hard work of the population were and are the main forces behind the economic development of Budapest. After the accommodation with Austria in 1867, Budapest was chosen as the capital and became the site of important industrial enterprises. The industrial combine

Development

Trade and Industry

Ganz (locomotives, machinery, wagons, cranes, ships, etc.) was developed from a foundry established in the middle of the previous century. In 1868 Lázlo Láng from Pressburg laid the foundation of an undertaking which is now the most important combine of eastern Europe. The present-day iron and metal works Csepel, the products of which range from steel pipes to sewing-machines, was founded by B. M. Weiss in 1893.

Between the two world wars, tool-making, telecommunications and textile manufacture gave a new economic impetus to the city. After the Second World War there was further extension of industry. The provision of raw materials from the USSR made possible not only an extension of capacity for existing branches of industry, but also the setting up of works for the oil and chemical industries. For some time now the Ikarus factory has been in a position to supply buses not only to the countries in eastern Europe, but also to Western customers. Since the 1960s, when the top-heavy nature of Hungarian industry was first recognised, more and more factories have been moved outside the conurbation of Budapest.

Trade Fairs

As one of the leading centres of trade fairs in eastern Europe, Budapest plays a major part in national and international exhibitions and congresses. The necessary space requirements are being met, particularly by the extension of the existing exhibition centre HUNGEXPO in District X. A modern congress centre was opened in 1985 near the South Station.

Among the important extra regional and regular trade fairs, are the international fairs in May and September/October, BNV (Budapesti Nemzetközi Vásár), as well as the tourist exhibition UTAZAS in March.

Banks

Thanks to its strong economy, Budapest is one of the leading finance centres of eastern Europe. Even a number of Western institutions have set up branches in Budapest, among them the National City Bank of Minneapolis, the Banque Nationale de Paris, the Banco di Sicilia, the Central European International Bank and also the Austrian Creditanstalt Bankverein.

Tourism

The historic spa of Budapest has developed in the past ten years into one of the most important tourist centres in Europe. The majority of the 18 million tourist who came to Hungary in 1988 paid a visit to Budapest. Visitors from Western countries (especially Austria, West Germany, Italy, the Netherlands, Switzerland, the USA and Canada) brought the most foreign currency into the city.

Today there are more than 18,000 beds available in more than 60 sizeable hotels. New luxury hotels are either in the planning stage or are already being built. However, the numbers of people who can be accommodated are signicantly higher if you include simple boarding-houses and private rooms to let.

Trade

Budapest's favourable geographical position, in terms of communications, means that it has long been a centre of trade. This is especially true of the city area of Pest, where today all lines of Hungarian economic management converge. In addition, within the sphere of the countries of eastern Europe, Budapest has a leading place as a shopping centre. More than a dozen large stores and numerous other shops and boutiques between the Danube Quay and the Outer Ring offer a wide range of goods. The central markets of the Hungarian capital are no different from those in Western cities.

Notable Personalities

Árpád, tribal prince of the Magyars who belong to the Finno-Ugrian ethnic group, led his people who moved westwards from an area between the Volga and the Kama, over the Carpathians into present-day Hungary, in about 896.

Árpád
Tribal Prince of the Magyars
(c. 880–907)

Béla Bartók, born in Nagyszentmiklós, is with Franz Liszt and Zoltán Kodály among the most famous Hungarian composers. For many years a Professor of Music in Budapest, he made a name for himself as an impulsive champion of the "new music". His rhythms, chords and melodies are evidence of a keen understanding and knowledge of Hungarian popular music. Bartók did not only write piano pieces, he also composed for orchestras and chamber ensembles. Among his best-known works are the opera "Count Bluebeard's Castle" and the ballet "The Wonderful Mandarin".

Béla Bartók
Composer
(25.3.1881–26.9.1945)

This politician, born in Sojtor, led the moderate liberals of the Reform movement in 1848. After 1849 he led the Address Party (so called from the address which this group made to the Austrian Emperor Franz Joseph), on the initiative of which the accommodation with Austria followed in 1867. This led to the establishment of the Austro-Hungarian monarchy.

Ferenc (Francis) von Deák
Politician and Lawyer
(17.10.1803–29.1.1876)

The Baron, a native of Buda was one of the spiritual leaders of the Hungarian Reform movement of the 1840s. He was twice Minister of Culture and Education (1848 in the Batthyány Cabinet and again in 1867 after the Austro-Hungarian accommodation); he campaigned for the extension of Hungarian primary school education and for equal rights for religious denominations.
In his novels Eötvös dealt with the social conditions of his age.

József (Joseph)
Baron of Eötvös
Writer and Politician
(13.9.1813–2.2.1871)

Loránd of Eötvös, the son of Jozsef Baron of Eötvös, is one of the great personalities to come out of Budapest, where he worked as a Professor of Physics and from 1894 to 1895 was Hungarian Minister of Culture. He became world famous through his studies into the theory of gravitation (the Eötvös effect) and the construction of a new kind of rotary balance.

Loránd (Roland) of Eötvös
Physicist
(27.7.1848–8.4.1919)

Ferenc Erkel, who was born in Békésgyula and who died in Budapest, is one of the best-known composers of his fatherland. Not only did he write the melody of the old Hungarian National Anthem, but also the work "Hunyadi Lászlo" which found a place in the history of music as the Hungarian national opera.

Ferenc (Francis) Erkel
Composer
(7.11.1810–15.6.1893)

Greatly venerated in Hungary, St Gellért was a Benedictine monk and sometime Abbot of the Monastery of St Giorgio in Venice. King Stephen I brought him into the country of the Magyars in order that he should instruct his son Emmerich. In about 1030 Gellért became the first Bishop of Csanád. He died in Buda as a martyr and was canonised in 1083.

Szent Gellért
(St Gerhard of Csanád)
Bishop and Martyr
(?–24.9.1046)

The composer Károly Goldmark was born in Keszthely on Lake Balaton. As a composer of opera – his chief work is the "Queen of Sheba" – he was able to combine the ideas of Wagner with elements of French grand opera.

Károly (Karl) Goldmark
Composer
(18.5.1830–2.1.1915)

Notable Personalities

Ferenc von Deák

József von Eötvös

Mór Jókai

Gyula Illyés
Poet
(2.11.1902)

The poet Gyula Illyés, born in Rácegrespuszta, is one of the most important representatives of lyrical and narrative art of his native country. His work is inspired by influences of the French avant-garde. He is also important as a literary historian and the biographer of Petöfi.

Mór (Maurice) Jókai
Writer
(18.2.1825–5.5.1904)

Born in Komárom, he is considered to be the most important representative of the Romantic movement of Hungarian prose. His works comprise about 200 novels, narratives and short stories. Together with Petöfi he was the leader of the Reform-inspired youth movement of the year 1848 in Buda and Pest.

János Kádár
Politician
(26.5.1912–6.7.1989)

Born in Kapoly, this Communist politician was Hungarian Minister of the Interior from 1948 to 1950. In October 1956 he became a member of the Revolutionary Government of Nagy. As First Secretary of the newly formed Hungarian Socialist Workers' Party in 1956 he functioned, after the defeat of the popular uprising, as President from 1956 to 1958 and again from 1961 to 1965. Under his jurisdiction, measures of consolidation were introduced and led to a carefully controlled development of the economy which was to ensure a good position for Hungary within the COMECON group.

Imre Kálmán
Composer
(24.10.1882–30.10.1953)

Imre Kálmán was born in Siófok on the southern shore of Lake Balaton. He made a name as a composer of operetta and was celebrated as such not only in Budapest but also in Vienna and Paris. His best-known operettas are "The Gypsy Princess", "Countess Mariza", "The Circus Princess" and "The Duchess of Chicago".

Zoltán Kodály
Composer and Music Teacher
(16.12.1882–6.3.1967)

Born in 1882 in Kecskemét, Zoltán Kodály is the most important precursor of the Hungarian music movement which is oriented towards traditional popular music. Kodály worked principally in the Hungarian capital and today is one of the most respected Hungarian musicians. His unique collection of Hungarian folksongs is very famous.

Lajos (Louis) Kossuth
(19.9.1802–20.3.1894)

This lawyer, born in Monik (Komitat Zemplén), was the leading writer from 1840 to 1844 of the "Pesti Hirlap". He was one of the leading figures of the Hungarian liberals of the revolution year 1848/49 and instigated the break with the Viennese adminis-

Lajos Kossuth

Franz Liszt

Matthias Corvinus

tration. As Chairman of the Hungarian National Defence Committee he campaigned strongly for the Honvéd. In 1849 he had to resign his position as administrator of the Hungarian kingdom. He died in Turin.

Franz Liszt who was born in Raiding in Hungary, is today honoured as the most important son of the land of the Danube. He made his début as a concert pianist at the age of nine. He furthered his musical education in Vienna and Paris and in 1842 he was made Director of Music at the Court in Weimar. He was enobled in 1859. Between 1861 and 1869 he lived in Rome where he became head of the Hungarian Music Academy (today the Franz Liszt Music Academy), which had been founded at his instigation. As a composer he concentrated chiefly on symphonic writing, Church music and piano concerti. Among his most important works are the "Hungarian Rhapsodies", the "Années de Pélerinage", the "Hungarian Coronation Mass" and the "Gran Festival Mass". Franz Liszt was also revered as a teacher. Among his many pupils were a number of musicians who became well known, including Alexander Borodin and Friedrich Smetana.

Franz (Ferenc) Liszt
Composer and Pianist
(22.10.1811–31.7.1886)

Born in Budapest, this literary historian and philosopher was, in the time of the Hungarian-Soviet Republic, People's Commissar for Education. In 1945 he was made a professor. In the literary field Lukács gave most attention to the novel and realism. Today he is considered one of the leading Communist intellectuals.

Georg Lukács
Literary Historian and
Philosopher
(13.4.1885–4.6.1971)

Born in Klausenburg, the son of the Turkish conqueror Hunyadi, Corvinus was King of Hungary from 1458–1490. In 1469 he was crowned King of Bohemia. During his reign Buda developed into a leading cultural centre of the Renaissance. Italian painters and scholars worked at his Court. Mátyás I not only founded the Bibliotecha Corviniana, one of the greatest libraries in Europe at that time, he also set up a university in Pressburg and had the royal palace in Buda considerably extended. He died in 1490 in Vienna.

Mátyás (Matthias) I.
Corvinus
King of Hungary
(23.2.1443–6.4.1490)

Ferenc Molnár, born in Budapest, is the author of many widely read novels and short stories – among them an early novel "The Boys of St Paul's Street". His forte, however, was plays

Ferenc (Francis) Molnár
Writer
(12.1.1878–1.4.1952)

19

Notable Personalities

Sándor Petőfi

Ignác Semmelweis

Géza Graf Zichy

and comedies. Some of his pieces have been box-office hits round the world. Among the best known are "Liliom", "The Swan" and "Play in the Castle". There are many anecdotes and stories about Molnár who died in 1952 in New York.

Péter Pázmány
Archbishop
(4.10.1570–19.3.1637)

Péter Pázmány was born in Grosswardein. In his youth he was brought up as a Calvinist but in 1583 he became a Catholic. In 1616 he became Archbishop of Esztergom and led the Hungarian Counter-Reformation. Also known as a man of letters, he founded the University of Tyrnau in 1635 and this was transferred to Buda under the Empress Maria Theresa.

Sándor (Alexander) Petőfi
Poet and Revolutionary
(1.1.1823–31.7.1849)

Some of the poems of this lyricist from Kiskőrős became known to a wide section of the public when he was only twenty-one years old. He was an ardent supporter of the Revolutionary movement of 1848/49. Petőfi composed the poem "Rise up Magyars!" which together with his various revolutionary songs was enthusiastically received. As the adjutant of the Polish General Bem he fought for freedom.

Ferenc (Francis) Rákóczi II
Hungarian Prince
(27.3.1676–8.4.1735)

Rákóczi, a nobleman born in Borsi, was in 1703 at the forefront of the fight for freedom of the Hungarians rebelling against the domination of the House of Habsburg. In 1704 he was elected Prince of Siebenburgen and one year later Prince of Hungary. His freedom movement was defeated and so Rákóczi felt obliged to flee to Turkey. He died in Rodosto on the Sea of Marmara.

Ignác (Ignatius) Philipp
Semmelweis
Physician
(1.7.1818–13.8.1865)

A native of Buda, Semmelweis was a doctor and obstetrician who has gone down in medical history as "the saviour of mothers". He acquired this reputation by discovering the cause of and combating puerperal fever.

István (Stephen) I
King of Hungary
(c. 975–15.8.1038)

István, a scion of the Arpáds and the Patron Saint of Hungary, was created King of Hungary at Christmas in the year 1000 with a Crown remitted to him by Pope Sylvester II. He organised a feudal State on the French model. He replaced the old tribal constitution by a county administration. The seat of his government was Gran (Esztergom), where he founded an archbishopric in about 1000. István I was made a saint in 1083.

Pál (Paul) Szabó. Writer
(20.3.1894–2.11.1970)

Pál Szabó, who worked for many years in Budapest, is one of the leading representatives of Hungarian literature. In 1960 he became Vice-president of the International PEN Club. Among his best-known works are "People" and "Liberated Country".

Count Széchenyi is one of the forerunners of the Hungarian Reform movement of the last century. He opposed the freedom from taxation enjoyed by the nobility, demanded the repeal of the guilds and became a champion of the peasantry. He was the founder of the Hungarian Academy of Science and a pioneer of the Danube Steamship Company; in 1848 he became the Minister of Transport in Hungary.

István (Stephen), Count Széchenyi
Politician
(21.9.1792–8.4.1860)

Born in Budapest, the conductor Széll studied in Vienna and with Reger in Leipzig. He worked in Berlin, Glasgow, New York and Cleveland and was also popular in Salzburg as a guest conductor.

Georg Széll
Conductor
(7.6.1897–31.7.1970)

This Professor of Geography in Budapest became the Hungarian Foreign Minister in 1920 and President from 1920 to 1921. In 1939 he was again named President and conducted the second arbitration with Vienna. He committed suicide when he was unable to prevent the entry of his homeland into the Second World War.

Pál (Paul) Teleki
Geographer and Politician
(1.11.1879–3.4.1941)

Mihály Vörösmarty was one of the most important representatives of Hungarian poetry at the time of the Reform. In his work "Zalans Flight", which appeared in 1900 and was written in German, he glorified the acquisition of land by the Magyars. His "Aufruf" (rallying call) was elevated to the status of a national anthem.

Mihály (Michael) Vörösmarty
Poet
(1.12.1800–19.11.1855)

Born in Sztára the Count was descended from the old Hungarian aristocratic line of Zichy zu Zich and Vásony-Keö. Although he had lost his right arm at the early age of fourteen in a hunting accident, he studied music and by sheer hard work eventually, as one of Franz Liszt's pupils, became a virtuoso pianist with the left hand. In addition he created his own compositions such as operas (including in 1905–12 a trilogy about the Hungarian national hero Rákóczi), choral works, songs and piano music as well as solo pieces and studies for the left hand. Zichy became President of the Hungarian National Conservatoire and Administrator of the Hungarian Opera House in Budapest.

Géza Count Zichy
Composer
(23.7.1849–14.1.1924)

21

History of Budapest

Old Stone Age	The earliest known traces of settlements on the Buda bank of the Danube.
Middle and New Stone Age	Numerous finds confirm a continuous human activity on the Buda side of the Danube.
2nd c. B.C.	Both banks of the Danube are settled.
Bronze Age	In the entire area of the present-day Hungarian capital several urn sites have been uncovered.
6th c. B.C.	Nomadic Scythian tribes from the area of the Black Sea settle in the area of Budapest.
4th–3rd c. B.C.	Celtic Eraviscs emerge as settlers.
2nd c. A.D.	The Roman fortress of Aquincum, situated in what is now the district of Obuda, becomes the capital of the Province of Pannonia Inferior. Aquincum, which was divided into a military town and a civil town, reached its heyday at the end of the 2nd c.
5th c.	The Huns capture Aquincum. King Attila (Etzel) sets up a great kingdom.
6th–9th c.	The Avars settle by the Danube.
c. 896	The Magyars belonging to the Finno-Ugrian ethnic group led by Prince Arpád press upstream along the Danube from the Carpathians and settle in the area of present-day Obuda.
1000	István (Stephen) I becomes King of Hungary. He organises a feudal State on the Central European model and introduces Christianity. His residences are at Esztergom (Gran) and Székesfehérvár.
12th c.	Merchants from central and west Europe settle in Buda and Pest.
1241–42	Mongols storm the rising Danube cities of Buda and Pest.
1270	Construction of the Castle of Buda ordered by King Béla IV is completed.
1255	Buda receives a market charter.
14th c.	The House of Anjou inherits the Hungarian throne.
1342–82	Lajos (Louis) I (the Great) reigns as king. He has a magnificent palace erected on Castle Hill. Under his leadership the Hungarian sphere of influence extents to Bosnia, Serbia, Bulgaria and into Wallachia.
1387–1437	Sigismund of Luxemburg, later the German Emperor, reigns in Hungary.

St Stephen's crown, orb and sceptre

Mátyás Hunyadi (Matthias Corvinus), son of the Turkish conqueror János Hunyadi, is King of Hungary. During his reign Buda develops into a centre of Renaissance culture. The Royal Palace in Buda is extended. With the Bibliotheca Corviniana, one of the greatest libraries of Europe is established.	1458–90
György Dózsa assembles a peasant army outside Pest with the object of attacking the despotic rule of the nobility.	1514
After their victory over the Hungarian troops at Mohács, the Turks temporarily occupy the Castle of Buda.	1526
Under Sultan Süleyman I (the Magnificent) the Turks control Buda and Pest. At this period many churches are converted into mosques, defensive works renewed and fine bath-houses constructed. Buda is the seat of a Vizier.	1541–1686
Charles of Lorraine retakes Óbuda, Buda and Pest for the House of Habsburg.	1686
Resistance against the rule of the Habsburg Emperor of Vienna.	End 17th/beginning 18th c.
Various measures taken by the Empress Maria Theresa lead to a modest economic upsurge. In the meantime a considerable number of German-speaking settlers arrive in Buda and Pest.	1740–80
Bloody defeat of the Hungarian Jacobins.	1795
The University of Tyrnau (Nagyszombat) is moved to Buda. It is the only college of its kind in Hungary. Seven years later it is transferred to Pest.	1797

History of Budapest

1825	Foundation of a scientific society as the precursor of the now famous Hungarian Academy of Science.
1837	Building of the National Theatre.
1838	After a disasterous flood of the Danube there follows a comprehensive redevelopment.
1st half 19th c.	Pest becomes a thriving economic centre where trade in grain flourishes in particular.
1848–49	Civil revolution led by liberal nobles and a struggle for freedom against the Austrian hegemony. Count Lajos Batthyány forms a Hungarian government responsible to the State's Parliament. Lajos Kossuth rises to be the most important political leader; the poet Sándor Petőfi, a fervent revolutionary, dies during the struggle for freedom.
1849	The Chain Bridge is opened to traffic.
1867	Accommodation with the ruling Austrian house through the mediation of Ferenc Deák. Emperor Franz Joseph II is crowned King of Hungary in Matthias Church. The Austro-Hungarian monarchy of the Danube comes into being.
1872	Óbuda, Buda and Pest are combined into a city.
1887	The first tram runs in Budapest.
1896	Festivities marking the 1000-year existence of Hungary.
1902	The Parliament Building is completed.
Beginning of the 20th c.	A considerable number of industrial undertakings are established in Budapest. The contours of a "Ruhr district by the Danube" are drawn up.

Old drawing of Buda and Pest in 1617

Economic and social defects lead to unrest which culminates in strikes and demonstrations; on 23 May, "blood-red Thursday", these are ended by force.	1912
First World War. Budapest suffers severe setbacks in its economic development.	1914–18
The Republic is proclaimed.	16.11.1918
A Soviet Republic, established in March and supported by Social Democrats and Communists is only able to last for a few months. In November Miklós Horthy seizes power.	1919
First transmission of Budapest Radio.	1925
Large workers' demonstrations.	1930
Hungary enters the Second World War on the side of Germany.	1941
The turmoil of war influences life in the Hungarian capital. Horthy is locked up by the National Socialists. In autumn Budapest becomes a front-line town and suffers severe damage, especially in the castle quarter where units of the German army are barricaded in.	1944
From now on Soviet units control the whole of Budapest.	13.2.1945
The Freedom Bridge is opened to traffic.	1946
The new Hungarian constitution comes into force. 20 August becomes a national holiday.	20.8.1949

View from Castle Hill over the Danube

History of Budapest

1950	By a administrative reform the area of Budapest is considerably extended. Opening of the Ferihegy Airport.
1953	Completion of the Nép Stadium. Imre Nagy becomes prime minister of Hungary
1955	Nagy is forced out of office by the Stalinists
1956	In October Imre Nagy becomes prime minister of a coalition government. He opposes the existing system of government and declares Hungary's neutrality. Political and economic abuses fuel a popular uprising in autumn. This leads to heavy fighting between the rebels and the Government troops and with Soviet units. The inner city presents a picture of devastation. János Kádár, First Secretary of the newly founded Workers' Party, introduces measures of consolidation and gives an impulse for a carefully increased development of the economy.
1958	The former prime minister Imre Nagy is executed for high treason.
1964	The Elisabeth Bridge is opened to traffic.
1960–80	Development of a comprehensive programme of civic building and extension of the local transport system (especially the Underground network).
from 1975	Exemplary renovation of the old city centre of Buda (in particular the castle quarter) and Pest. Opening of several large luxury hotels.
1983	Budapest is the venue for the world gymnastic championships.
1984	The sixth full assembly of the World Lutheran Federation.
1985	KSZE – Culture forum.

Parliament Building overlooking the Danube

COMECOM conference attended by Mr Gorbachev.   1986

European regional conference.   1987

World figure-skating and ice-dancing championships are held   1988
in Budapest.
Some 20,000 Hungarians demonstrate against a proposed
power station on the Danube north of Budapest.
A large number of Romanian refugees settle, temporarily at
least, in Budapest.

Prime minister Németh and party chief Grósz declare them-   1989
selves in favour of more democracy. The events of 1956 are
viewed in a fresh light. On 16 June hundreds of thousands pay
homage to the former prime minister Imre Nagy who, together
with some of his colleagues, was executed exactly 31 years
ago.
The "Iron Curtain" on the Hungaro-Austrian border is pulled
down. Several thousand East Germans take advantage of the
situation to flee to Austria and West Germany.

Budapest from A to Z

Short stays
Suggestions on how best to spend a short stay in Budapest will be found under "Practical Information – Sightseeing Programme" at the back of this book.

Museum opening times
As the opening times of museums often change in Hungary it is not possible, in spite of all our efforts, to keep these up-to-date. To avoid a wasted journey, therefore, we recommend checking these on the spot.

Academy of Music

See Franz Liszt Academy of Music

Academy of Science

See Roosevelt tér

Academy Utca

Roosevelt tér

Agricultural Museum

See City Woodland Park

Alagút

See Chain Bridge

Alfréd Hajós Baths

See Margaret Island

Allami Opera House

See State Opera

◀ *Matthias Church in Buda*

Angyalföld

Underground Station
M3 (Elmunkás tér)

Trams
3V, 12, 14, 33V, 55, 75, 76, 79

Buses
4, 15, 20, 26, 30, 32, 33, 43,
43A, 55, 84, 120

The district of Angyalföld, lying in the north of Pest was, until the Second World War, a sombre industrial suburb. Since the 1950s a modern district has arisen here.
By the busy Elmunkás tér stands the Church of St Margaret built in 1922 by István Möller. Behind lies a large market. Farther to the north the Attila József Theatre (1950; Váci út 63) can be found.
A monument commemorating the poet József Attila (1955 by A. Beck) stands on József Attila Square.

Nép-sziget Danube Island

The Island of Nép-sziget in the Danube off Angyalföld is principally used for relaxation and recreation. Rowing regattas often take place in the blocked-off arm of the Danube.

Szabadság-fürdő

See Practical Information, Spas.

Anjou Bastion

See Buda, Important Streets and Squares, Bécsi kapu tér

Anonymous Monument

See City Woodland Park

Aquincum

See Óbuda

Archduke Joseph Square

See József Nádor tér

Árpád Bridge (Árpád-hid)

Location
Obuda-Angyalföld

Underground Station
M3 (Árpád-hid)

Tram
1

Almost 1 km in length and the most northerly of the Budapest road bridges, Árpád Bridge which crosses the northern tip of Margaret Island (see entry), links the districts of Buda and Angyalföld (see entries). Its construction was begun in 1939 and it was opened to traffic in 1950.
Additional construction work since 1983 has made the bridge an important link in the road system of Budapest.

Art Gallery

See Heroes' Square

Artists' Promenade

See Margaret Island

Bajcsy-Zsilinszky út

See Inner Ring

Basilica

See St Stephen's Basilica

Batthyány Palace

See Outer Ring, Lenin körút

Batthyány tér

See Viziváros

Bécsi kapu tér

See Buda, Important Streets and Squares

Béla-Komjádi Swimming Pool

See Imperial Baths and Luke's Baths

Béla-Lajta House

See Martinelli tér

Bem József tér

See Viziváros

Biermann István tér

See Martinelli tér

Blaha Lujza tér

See Outer Ring

Botanical Garden of the University (Füvészkert) G6

Location
Korányi Sándor u.

Underground Station
M3 (Nagyvárad tér)

Tram
24

Bus
33

Laid out in 1847, and originally quite extensive, the Botanical Garden of the University became more and more restricted in size by the continuing extension of built-up areas in the Hungarian capital. In the garden, which is also considered a place for relaxation, more than 7000 different species of plants can be found. The early classic administration building dating from 1802 is noteworthy.

In the vicinity of the Botanical Garden are some of the extensive buildings of the University Hospital.

**Buda B/C4/5(K–N6–8)

Location
On the right bank of the Danube

Buses
V, 5, 16, 16A, 86

Funicular Railway
Clark Adám tér–Szent György tér

In the 13th c. the Hungarians, under their King Béla IV, realised the strategic importance of the water-bearing strata of the wedge-shaped Pleistocene lone hill (168 m (550 ft high)) on the right bank of the Danube. On its south-east point they built Castle Buda, which was soon to be made a residence of the Hungarian kings. On the castle plateau and parallel to it a royal city arose, which for a long time was to become the brilliant focal point of the country and the Danube. Buda, which quickly began to extend down the slope (see Víziváros), fused with the neighbouring Óbuda on the north and in 1872 was joined with Óbuda and Pest to become the city of Budapest.

The heart of old Buda has kept its charm. Its numerous architectural monuments, which were lovingly rebuilt and restored after the devastation of the Second World War, attract thousands of visitors every year.

Buda and the section of the Danube which belongs to it have, for some time now, been included in the UNESCO list of protected cultural centres.

Walkman Guide

In the office of Budapest Tourist (I. Szentháromság utca 5; tel. 736–732) you can hire a Walkman Guide for a small fee. With its help you can get to know the Castle Quarter in about one and a half hours.

Castle Palace

See entry

Matthias Church

See entry

Fishermen's Bastion

See entry

Important Streets and Squares in Buda

Bécsi kapu tér (Vienna Gate Square)

The Saturday Market was formerly held in the square by the north gate (Vienna Gate) of the castle quarter. On the inside of the Vienna Gate, restored in 1936, a tablet commemorates the liberation of Buda from the Turks in 1686. In front of the gate, as a symbol of the victory of 1686, is "Angel with the Cross", by B. Ohmann (1936). Several buildings frame the Bécsi kapu tér; the Lutheran Church (Evangélikus-templom; 1895; concerts in summer), the huge National Archive (Országos Levéltár; 1917) in Neo-Romanesque style, as well as a number of Baroque and Classical dwellings. To the east of the gate lies the Europark (Európa-liget), laid out in 1973, and to the west the Anjou Bastion (Anjou-bástya). Near by is the memorial to the last Turkish Pasha of Buda.

This square, which is surrounded by several Baroque and Classical buildings, was a market-place in the Middle Ages. In the centre stands a Honvéd statue by G. Zala (1893) which commemorates the War of Liberation of 1848/49.

Disz tér (former Parade Ground)

To the south to one side of Disz tér, stands the recently renovated Castle Theatre; the building was destroyed in the Second World War. It is housed in a monastic complex converted in 1787 by F. Kempelen. The first theatrical performance in the Hungarian language took place here in 1790.

Várszínház (Castle Theatre)

The Sándor Palace is being reconstructed near the Castle Theatre.

Sándor-palota (Sándor Palace)

Fortuna Street was so called at the end of the 18th c. after the Fortuna Inn (No. 4; now the Museum of Commerce and Catering). It is characterised by numerous buildings in the finest Baroque and later styles. In the Middle Ages many French craftsmen lived here.

Fortuna utca (Fortuna Street)

Andreas Hess Square is named after the first printer of books in Buda (1473) and is embellished with a statue of Pope Innocent XI, a work by J. Danko (1936). Medieval remains on the east side of the square were cleverly incorporated a few years ago into the architecture of the highly modern luxury hotel, the Budapest Hilton (where the Budapest Casino is situated). Among the important relics are the St Nicholas Tower (Miklóstorony), and the remains of the Late Gothic Church of St Nicholas of the Dominicans, who had a large monastery here as early as the 13th c. A copy of the Matthias Corvinas Reliefs, which is incorporated in the hotel, depicts the highly esteemed King of the Hungarians. Behind the Innocent Monument is the architectural complex the Red Hedgehog (Vörös sun ház) which dates from the 17th–18th c. and which was later remodelled in Classical style.

Hess András tér (Andreas Hess Square)

Kapisztrán Square is situated in the north-west of the castle quarter. It is named after Johannes Capistranus, a forerunner of the Turkish conqueror János Hunyadi. A monument to him by J. Damko (1922) is to be seen outside the Museum of Military History (Hadtörténeti Intézet és Múzeum; documents and various exhibits about the military history of Hungary). On the south side of the square there stood, until the Second World War, the Church of St Mary Magdalene (Mária Magdolna-templom; 13th–15th c.) but only the Gothic tower now remains.

Behind the Museum of Military History the Anjou Bastion in the Esztergom Round Tower adjoins the wall protecting the south-west side of Castle Hill and the battlements (Tóth Arpád sétány)

The Kapistrán memorial

Buda

Budapest Hilton (Danube facade)

Plague Column (Szentháromság tér)

which extend round it. From here there is a fine view of the western parts of Budapest and the Buda Hills.

Országház utca
(Parliament Street)

Országház utca is the principal street of the castle quarter. In the northern part of Parliament Street, Baroque architecture is especially shown to advantage, but in the southern part Gothic predominates. Here and there Gothic and Renaissance elements (for instance houses Nos. 2 and 10) can still be found. The buildings of Nos. 18–22 date from the 15th century but have been remodelled since then several times. The former Monastery of St Clare (No. 28), founded in the Middle Ages, was rebuilt by F. A. Hillebrandt in the 18th century. Theareafter it was the home of the State Parliament and the High Court of the Hungarian capital. The great hall of this historic and interesting building has been splendidly restored; here functions of the Hungarian Academy of Science and concerts are held from time to time.

Szedntháromság tér
(Trinity Square)

The central square in the castle quarter is the Szentháromság tér with a large Baroque plague column designed by Barbier and Ungleich (1714). On the east side of the square stands the Matthias Church (see entry), on the north side the Finance Ministry which was built between 1901 and 1904 by A. Fellner. On the corner of Szentháromság tér and Szentháromság utca is the former Town Hall of Buda, now the home of the Linguistic Institute of the Hungarian Academy of Science. It was built in the 17th–18th c. from plans by the Italian architect Ceresola and was later extended along the Uri utca. Below the oriel balcony of the former Town Hall can be seen "Pallas Athene" by Carlo

Adami (1795). The courtyard and the staircase are also of great architectural and historical interest.

In the little Szentháromság utca which leads from Trinity Square to the west wall of the castle quarter is the Ruszwurm Café (Ruszwurm cukrászda; No. 7) which has been there since 1827 and where a predecessor stood in the Middle Ages. Near by is an equestrian statue (G. Vastagh; 1937) to Andreas Hadik who was raised to the rank of field-marshal by the Empress Maria Theresa.

Szentháromság utca
(Trinity Street)

Táncsics Milhály utca, the street where numerous Jews once lived, leads from Hess András tér to Bécsi kapu tér. Two of the fine Baroque buildings here are the Erdőly-Palais (No. 7; 1769) and No. 23 which stands on medieval foundations. Near by are the remains of an old synagogue. The prayer-house of the Jewish community of Buda (No. 26; museum) was founded in the 15th c.

Táncsics Milhály utca
(Mihaly-Tancsics Street)

Tárnoc utca, formerly a busy shopping street, leads from Trinity Square to Disz tér. The most architecturally important buildings, some of which are still medieval but with Baroque and Classical elements, are at present being renovated. The Arany Sas-patika (Golden Eagle Pharmacy; No. 18) which has stood since the 18th c. is now furnished as a pharmaceutical museum.

Tárnoc utca
(Treasurers' Street)

Romanesque, Gothic and Baroque architecture are features of Uri utca. The fine vaulting and the sedilia in the entrance of No. 40 are impressive. From No. 9 there is a way through to the maze of caves and subterranean passages in the area of Castle Hill.

Uri utca
(Gentlemen's Street)

*Budafok (formerly Promonter)

The scenically charming district of Budafok in the south of the Hungarian capital on the right bank of the Danube was famous up to the second half of the 19th c. for its viticulture. A maze of wine cellars and subterranean tunnels still show evidence of its former reputation.

Station
Budafok–Belváros

Trams: 14, 41

Buses: 3, 14, 58, 172

A particularly charming Baroque church stands in the old village square; it was completed in 1756. Features of the interior are an altar-painting by Altomonte and a pulpit in Rococo style. Also of note are sculptures dating from the time when the church was built.
Near the church, Péter-Pál utca goes uphill and along it a number of buildings from former centuries have been preserved.
In the cemetery of Budafok, south-west of the church, there are beautiful Baroque and Classical tombstones.

Baroque church

The headquarters of the National Wine Producers (Allami pincegazdaságok; Kossuth Lajos utca 84) and the Budafok Wine Producers (Budafoki Pincegazdaság) still make use of part of the considerable network of cellars and tunnels. A wine cellar furnished in the traditional manner is the Borkatakomba (Nagytétényi út 63).
Many of the cellars were at one time lived in. This is very clearly demonstrated in the cellar in Veréb u. 4.

Wine Cellars (viewing by appointment)

Budapest Historical Museum

See Castle Palace

*Buda Upland (Budai-hegység)   A1–8(K/L1/2)

Location
To the west of the town

Cog-wheel Railway
Város major–Széchenyi-hegy

Chair-lift
Zugliget–János-hegy

Three Frontier Hill
(Hármashatár-hegy)

János-hegy
(John's Hill)

The Buda Upland forms the natural western boundary of the Hungarian capital. The hills, consisting of dolomite, chalk, clay and marl are, for the most part, wooded and have long been popular as a local recreation area with the inhabitants of Budapest. A close network of paths, fine scenery, facilities for games and sports, a pioneer railway, cafés, etc., testify to the attractions of this beautiful upland area.
Buses: D, H, J, 28, 29, 65, 158.

The Three Frontier Hill (497 m (1631 ft)) rises to the north within the boundary of Budapest. From its almost bare summit there is a fine view of Óbuda. Below the top of the hill to the north-east can be seen the strange Guckler rock (Guckler-szikla). Two kilometres (1 mile) north-north-west (as the crow flies) from the Three Frontier Hill rises Csúcs-hegy (445 m (1460 ft); good view). Below to the south in Paul's Valley is a stalactitic cave (Pálvögyi cseppköbarlang) which is well worth visiting.

János-hegy rises in the west of Buda. It is the highest eminence in the Hungarian capital (529 m (1736 ft)). From the almost 24 m (79 ft) high observation tower (built in 1910) there is a magnificent view. János-hegy has also been made attractive for

View of Széchenyi-hegy and television tower

winter-sports enthusiasts by the installation of a chair-lift, a ski-jump, a piste and a ski-lift.

In the west of the city stands Freedom Hill, once known as the Swabian Mountain. During the Turkish Wars there was an army camp here. Over the years, well-to-do inhabitants of Budapest have settled here. Today it is a smart area with fine villas, the result of the industrial boom, and unltra-modern bungalows. From Városmajor Park (see entry) a cog-wheel railway, which was planned in the 19th c., ascends Szabadság-hegy and Széchenyi-hegy (439 m (1441 ft); transmitter of Hungarian Television). Up here are several nursing-homes and tourist hotels.

Szabadság-hegy (Freedom Hill) and Széchenyi-hegy

A narrow-gauge pioneer railway opened in 1951 and staffed by children and young people under the supervision of adults, provides an excursion into this especially charming scenic part of the Buda Upland.

Pioneer railway

Café Gerbeaud

See Vörösmarty tér

Café Hungária

See Outer Ring, Lenin körút

Café Ruszwurm

See Buda, Important Streets and Squares, Szentháromság utca

Calvin Square

See Inner Ring, Kálvin tér

Castle

See Buda
See Castle Palace

Castle Museum

See Castle Palace

Castle Museum Nagytétény

See Nagytétény

**Castle Palace (Várpalota)

C5(M/N8)

The magnificent Castle Palace of Buda, the origins of which go back to the 13th c., occupies the southern spur of Castle Hill.

Location
South spur of Castle Hill

Buda

Várpalota Castle Palace

PALACE WING

A   Museum of the Hungarian Workers' Movement

B
C   } National Gallery
D

E   Budapest Historical Museum (Castle Museum)

F   Széchenyi National Library

St George's Square

King Matthias's Fountain

Prince Eugene

Magazine Room

North Gate in defensive wall

Castle Chapel

Inner Ward

Well

South Gate in defensive wall

Gothic Hall

Murder Corridor

Outer Ward

Ferdinand's Gate

Buzogány Tower

South Round Tower

Lihegő Gate tower

Turkish graves

MEDIEVAL ROYAL PALACE

1   South Courtyard
2   Beatrix Court
3   Museum entrance
4   Ante-room of the Cellar Floor
5   Ante-room of Albrecht Cellar
6   Albrecht Cellar Cisterna regia
7   Ice hole
8
9   } Underground vaults
10
11   St Stephen's Tower
12   Renaissance Hall
13   Passage
14   Connecting passage
15   Royal Cellar
16   Oriel
17   Upper Cellar
18   Corvina Cellar
19   Ante-room of the Lower Chapel
20   Lower Chapel

300 m
330 yds

The extensive buildings, from which there are excellent views, are the former residence of the Hungarian kings, but they were severely damaged in the Second World War, and lengthy rebuilding was necessary. A great part of the palace buildings today appear in new splendour and provide room for important museums and other cultural facilities.

The first castle was built by King Béla IV in the 13th c. Its purpose was to provide protection from attacks by Tartars and Mongols. Unfortunately nothing remains of this building.
Under King Karl Robert a smaller palace was erected in the 14th c. King Sigismund, who made Buda his residence, had a Gothic castle built, which was considerably extended, in Renaissance style, under Matthias Corvinus.
Although the Castle Palace remained during the time of Turkish occupation, it was nevertheless ruined during the Siege of 1686. Therefore, in the 18th c. a new castle was built, which in the time of the Empress Maria Theresa had more than 200 rooms. The Castle Palace, from now on the residence of the Palatine (the representative of the Habsburg overlords), was rebuilt by the architects Hauszmann and Ybl in Neo-Baroque style. A symmetrical layout was created which is oriented to the central dome facing the Danube.

Buses
16, 16A

Funicular Railway
Clark Adám tér–Szent
György tér

History of the building

Cave System in the Castle Hill, Panopticum

In days gone by a vast system of caves was dug in the castle hill. This subterranean network is about 24 m/80 ft in length. The German army was able to hold out here for a long time at the end of the Second World War.
A waxworks (panopticum) has been installed in part of the cave-system, portraying in words and pictures the history of the Magyars from prehistoric times until the Renaissance.

Entrance
1, Úri utca 9

Opening times
Tues.–Sun. 10 a.m.–5 p.m.

Admission fee

Museum of the Hungarian Workers' Movement
(Magyar Munkásmozgalmi Múzeum; Wing A)

Since 1977 the Museum of the Hungarian Workers' Movement has been housed in the northern wing A. It contains interesting documents, materials and objects from workshops as well as furnishings from workers' dwellings which illustrate the life and the culture of the Hungarian workers since the middle of the 19th c.

Location
1, Dísz tér 17

Szent György tér (St George's Square)

In St George's Square stands a beautiful ornamental fountain designed by A. Stróbl; it shows King Matthias hunting.

*Hungarian National Gallery (Magyar Nemzeti Galéria; Wings B, C, D)

The Hungarian National Gallery occupies the three main wings of the castle and is still in the process of being built up. At the present time the following exhibits are to be seen:

Sculpture; frescoes; reproductions from the age of the foundation of the State; triptychs; sculptures and panels, including the

Location
1, Dísz tér 17

Romantic and Gothic

Hungarian National Gallery

Magyar Nemzeti Galéria

THIRD FLOOR

- Graphic Art
- Sculptures
- Graphic Art
- Coins and Small
- (19th–20th c.)
- Graphic Art
- Contemporary
- Temporary Exhibitions
- Temporary Exhibitions
- Work-shop
- 20th c. art

SECOND FLOOR

- of the
- Sculpture
- Museum shop
- 20th c.
- Exhibition
- Painting of the turn of the century
- Painting of the turn of the century
- Exhibition
- in preparation
- in preparation

FIRST FLOOR

- Painting
- Hungarian
- 20th c. art
- of the 19th c.
- 19th c. art
- Late Gothic triptychs, panels and sculptures
- Renaissance
- Hungarian Painting
- Late Renaissance, Baroque
- of the 19th c.

GROUND FLOOR

- Temporary exhibitions
- Temporary exhibitions
- 19th c. sculpture
- Temporary exhibitions
- Side entrance
- Cloakroom
- Information Ticket office
- Medieval sculpture
- Art of the Month'
- Information
- Medieval sculpture
- Ticket offices
- Gothic sculpture and panels
- Main entrance
- Lecture Hall

M Munkácsy ''Yawning apprentice'' (1868)   *and ''Woman churning butter'' (1873)*

Béla Uitz ''Woman in white'' (1918)   *Sándor Bortnyk: ''Red fabric'' (1919)*

Castle Palace

"Madonna Szlatvini", the "Madonna of Toporci" and the Altars of Jánosréti.

Renaissance

Sculpture, including the "Madonna of Diósgyori" and works of art from the Parish Church of the Inner City of Pest.

Late Renaissance and Baroque

Carving by Jakob Bogdány, Adám Mányoki as well as by Maulbertsch and his contemporaries; works of art of the Hungarian Age of Enlightenment; Late Baroque paintings and Baroque monumental sculpture.

19th c. paintings

Works by Károly Markó, Miklós Barabás, József Borsos, Géza Mészöly, Károly Lotz, Bertalan Székely, Merse Pál Szinyei, etc; paintings by Bálint Kiss, Viktor Madarász, Mór Than, Gyula Benczur, etc; separately but in chronological order: paintings by Mihály Munkácsy (including "Christ Before Pilate", "A Woman Collecting Faggots") and László Paál (especially landscapes).

19th c. sculpture

Works of art by Miklós Izsó, Alajos Stróbl, György Zala, János Fadrusz as well as some less-well-known masters.

Painting of the turn of the century

Paintings by Simon Hollosy, János Thoma, József Réti as well as works by members of the Nagybányai artists' colony (among them Károly Ferenczy).

20th c. painting

Well worth seeing is the collection of works painted since the turn of the century. Of particular importance are those by Béla Czóbel, József Egry, István Szőy and József Rippl-Rónai.

Coins and small sculptures

The numismatic collection and exhibition of small sculptures will prove very interesting. Both exhibitions are constantly being added to.

Graphical collection, naïve paintings

For some time now a part of the extensive graphical collection of the Hungarian National Gallery has been on display, together with some examples of naïve painting.

Temporary exhibitions

Special exhibitions are presented on various themes, to coincide with important cultural events in Budapest.

Equestrian Statue of Prince Eugene

In front of the domed building, on the side facing the Danube, is a bronze equestrian statue by József Róna (1900), representing Prince Eugene of Savoy who opposed the Turks.

Széchenyi National Library (Wing F)

The Széchenyi National Library has been in Wing F of the Castle Palace since 1985. This institution, founded by Count Ferenc Széchenyi in 1802, contains about 6 million books, more than 625,000 manuscripts and about 183,000 maps.
The highlight of the collection is the "Budapest Manuscripts", some of the oldest known medieval illuminated scripts.

Winged altar in the Castle chapel ▶

*Budapest Historical Museum

(Budapesti Történeti Múzeum; City Museum, Castle Museum; Wing E)

Location
1, György tér 2

Prince Eugene

Wing E of the Castle Palace houses the Budapest Historical Museum. It contains highly interesting documents, wrought-iron work, ceramics, textiles, household utensils and other objects which provide a comprehensive picture of the life and development of the Hungarian capital in the independent towns of Óbuda, Buda and Pest up to 1872.

In the ante-room of the basement is a model of the medieval Royal Palace. In the adjoining rooms of the medieval castle, partly reconstructed, can be seen sculpture and carving, stove tiles, kitchen utensils and weapons from the Royal Palace of the 14th and 15th c.

In the Renaissance Room is a picture showing Matthias Corvinus and Beatrice of Aragon, his second wife. The floor-tiles (majolica) are extremely beautiful. In the Gothic Room are fine sculptures dated 1370–1420. They were discovered during excavation work in 1874, and are some of the most interesting and beautiful examples of Gothic Hungarian sculpture. The "White Madonna" is outstanding. Other Gothic sculpture can be seen in the basement. A 14th c. triptych (see picture on p. 43) has been set up in the choir of the chapel. In the lower cellar are architectural elements also of the 15th c.

Remains of the Medieval Castle

Below Wings E and F of the Castle Palace parts of the medieval castle complex have been reconstructed. The Buzogány Tower (buzogány = morning star or club) is impressive as is the Ferdinand Gate. Outside is the South Tower which was in existence in the 15th and 16th c.

Outside the walls of the castle a number of Turkish tombstones can still be seen.

Castle Theatre

See Buda, Important Streets and Squares, Disz tér

Castle Vajdahunyad

See City Woodland Park

Castle Zichy

See Óbuda

Cella trichora

See Óbuda

Central Market Hall

See Dimitrov tér

Chain Bridge and Castle Palace after dark

Chain Bridge (Széchenyi-lánchid)

C5(N7)

The Chain Bridge, one of the landmarks of the Hungarian capital, was constructed between 1838 and 1849 by the English engineers William Tierny Clark and Adam Clark. The bridge, 375 m (410 yd) long and almost 16 m (18 yd) wide is supported by chains fixed to 48 m (158 ft) high towers at either end. At the ends of the bridge stand stone lions by J. Marschalkó. The bridge was destroyed in the Second World War, but in 1949 was again opened to traffic. It has recently been restored.
At the Buda end of the bridge lies Clark Adám tér, which in 1971 received the 0–km–stone by Miklós Borsos, the symbol from which distances along main roads from Budapest are measured.

Buses
2, 4, 16

From the Buda end of the Chain Bridge the Alagút, a road tunnel about 350 m (380 yd) long and which was constructed in 1857, leads to Krisztinaváros (Christian Town).
From the Buda end of the bridge tourists can also take the "Siklo" funicular railway up to the Castle Palace. This railway was built as long ago as 1870. After having "slumbered" for decades it has recently been restored.

Alagút

China Museum (Kina Múzeum)

F4

The China Museum in the Ráth villa and which developed from the China collection of the Ferenc-Hopp Museum of East-Asian Art (see entry), provides a good survey of Chinese art. Among

Location
Gorkij fasor 12

45

Circus

Trolleybuses
70, 78

Bus
33

the most beautiful exhibits, some of which are several hundred years old, are works of bronze, ivory and china. The textile collection is also of great interest.
Numerous visitors are attracted by the temporary exhibitions on various themes which are mounted throughout the year.
Opening times: Tues.–Sun. 10 a.m.–6 p.m.

Reformed Church
(Reformation templom)

Close at hand (Gorkij fasor 5–7) is the Reformed Church (1913; architect A. Arkay) in Secessionist style; the principal façade is decorated with beautiful majolica work.

Circus

See City Woodland Park, Civic Circus

Citadel

See Gellért Hill

City Museum

See Castle Palace, Budapest Historical Museum

*City Woodland Park (Városliget)   F/G3/4

Location
District XIV

Underground Station
M1 (Hősök tere, Széchenyi fürddő)

Trolleybuses
70, 72, 74, 75, 79

Buses
1, 4, 4A, 20, 30, 55

The Városliget (City Woodland Park) with its pretty lake, is the second largest of its kind in the Hungarian capital. Extending over more than 1 sq. km (0·8 sq. mile), the area was laid out in the 19th c. according to the ideas of the French landscape-gardener Nebbion. The Városliget has become a major attraction for the public through its cultural and recreational facilities – Zoological-Botanical Garden, pleasure park, Museum of Fine Art, art gallery, Civic Circus, Széchenyi Baths, Vajdahunyad Castle with the Agricultural Museum, Transport Museum, Arena Theatre, sports hall, games and sports grounds, garden for the blind.

*Castle Vajdahunyad (Vajdahunyad vára)   F3

Location
On the island in the lake

Opening times
Tues.–Sun. 10 a.m.–6 p.m.

The castle was built in 1896 by I. Alpár (monument outside the entrance) on the occasion of the millennium festival. In his work the architect tried to combine several architectural features which are characteristic of Hungary. The greater part of the building complex was designed on the model of the castle of the Turkish conqueror Hunyadi, which can be seen in the present-day Romanian town of Hunedoara.
The castle entrance has affinities with Gothic architecture; on the left it is flanked by a copy of a tower in Upper Hungary, on the right by a tower which is reminiscent of its model in Sighisoara in Romania. At the back of the Romanesque wing on the east side of the castle courtyard is a chapel, which was designed on the model of the Benedictine church in Jak in

Vajdahunyad Castle in the City Woodland Park

"Anonymous" Memorial,

Alpár Monument

western Hungary. Stylistic elements from north Hungary and Siebenburgen characterise the appearance of the part of the building on the right at the back of the castle entrance. A Renaissance wing forms a link with the palace in Baroque style which contains the Agricultural Museum.

Agricultural Museum

The Agricultural Museum (Mezőgazdasági Múzeum), housed in the Baroque Palace of Castle Vajdahunyad, provides a very good survey of the various facets of Hungarian agriculture. On show are implements of rural handcraft and machines for lightening the load of farming, documents about the raising of animals (especially horses, cattle, sheep and pigs), the production and storage of wine, forestry, as well as hunting (there is a fine collection of trophies) and fishing. Periodic special exhibitions complement the museum programme.
Opening times: Tues.–Sat. 10 a.m.–5 p.m., Sun. 10 a.m.–6 p.m.

Anonymous Monument

In the south-eastern courtyard of Castle Vajdahunyad stands a memorial, created in 1903 by Miklós Ligeti, honouring Anonymous, an unknown historical scribe of the 12th/13th c., who, it is believed, composed the first Hungarian chronicle.

Zoological-Botanical Garden (Fővárosi Allat-és Növénykert)   F3

Location
XIV, Allatkerti Körút 6–12

Trolleybus
72

The Budapest Zoological-Botanical Garden is situated in the north-west part of Városliget. It was laid out in the 1860s and has since been very popular with the citizens of Budapest.
Some of the indigenous and exotic animals (approximately 500 species) occupy enclosures in the open which were designed to resemble their natural habitat, as are the terrariums, aquariums and other purpose-made buildings. Among the attractions are the birds of prey cage, the rock garden, the polar bear and sealion pool, the children's zoo, the monkey house, the caves for lions and bears, the Africa house and the pachyderm house.
Interested visitors can study the flora of temperate latitudes along the paths; tropical plants can be found in the palm house as well as in the terrariums and aquariums for animals from hot countries.

Civic Circus (Fővárosi Nagycirkusz)   F3

Location
XIV, Allatkerti körút 7

Trolleybus
72

The new building of the Civic Circus, opened in 1971, is situated on the eastern edge of the zoo area, opposite the Széchenyi Baths; it is one of the most popular institutions of its kind in Europe. All the well-known circuses of the world have performed and still perform here. The circus tradition in Városliget goes back to 1891 when the first performances were staged.

Pleasure Park (Vidám Park)   F/G3

Location
XIV, Allatkerti körút 14–16

Trolleybus: 72

Every year many thousands of visitors come to the Budapest Tivoli, in the northern corner of the Városliget. This is a pleasure park with a giant wheel, a big dipper and various rides as well as numerous other diversions.

*Széchenyi Baths (Széchenyi-fürdő)   F3

Location
XIV, Allatkerti körút 11

The complex of the Széchenyi Baths in the northern part of Városliget comprises an open-air bath and a covered bath in

Neo-Baroque style with steam and normal baths. The warm water (over 70 °C (158 °F) comes from a spring discovered in the previous century.

Underground station
M1 (Széchenyi-fürdó)

Transport Museum (Közlekedési Múzeum)

G3

In a building constructed for the purpose in Városliget are the exhibits of the Hungarian Transport Museum. The development of transport from ancient times until today is very clearly portrayed. Models of old Danube and Lake Balaton vessels are included in the exhibition as are various locomotives and aircraft (record-breaking aircraft and helicopters). Outside the museum can be seen an old dining-car. In front of the museum is a children's area.

Location
XIV, Városligeti krt. 11

Trolleybus
72, 74

Opening times
Tues.–Sun. 10 a.m.–6 p.m.

Congress Centre

B6

Two kilometres (1·25 miles) south-west of the town, close to the Hotel Novotel Budapest, stands Hungary's first congress centre, opened in February 1985. The conference facilities (total area 10,756 sq. m/115,700 sq. ft, space for meetings 3000 sq. m/32,300 sq. ft), is designed according to the most modern ideas. The heart of the centre is the Patria Hall (1300 sq. m/14,000 sq. ft, with a maximum of 1750 seats), and with excellent acoustics.
Other halls and rooms are:
Bartok Hall (270 sq. m/2900 sq. ft, with 270 seats)
Palma Hall (130 sq. m/1400 sq. ft, 130 seats)
Corvina Room, Janus-Pannonius Room, Matyas Room (each being 30 sq. m/320 sq. ft, with seating for a maximum of 30)
Aula (560 sq. m/6025 sq. ft), and Chanson Hall (250 sq. m/2690 sq. ft).

Budapest Congress Centrum, tel: (361) 86 95 88.

Location
Hegyalja út 1–3

Tram
61

Buses
12, 112

Information

Contra Aquincum

See Március 15 tér

Corvin tér

See Viziváros

Csepel (Csepel-sziget)

Csepel, District XXI of the Hungarian capital, is situated on an island on the Danube and is the headquarters of the Csepel Vas-és Fémmüvek (Csepel Iron and Metal Works), with many thousand employees. This undertaking, established by B. M. Weiss in 1893 produces goods ranging from steel pipes to bicycles.

A modern Free Port lying on the west side of Csepel Island. The annual turnover of goods in this huge Free Port on the Danube is more than 3 million tonnes.

HEV stop
2 (Csepel)

Buses
38, 38A, 38B, 48, 51, 52, 52A, 59, 59A, 71, 148, 159

Szabadkiköto
(Free Port)

Danube

Csepel strandfürdő
(Swimming-bath)

The riverside swimming-bath of Csepel, fed by a thermal spring, is the third largest of its kind in Budapest. It is situated on the Soroksári Duna, a branch of the river on the east side of Csepel Island. Opposite lies the little island of Molnár-sziget.

*Danube

Boat Trips
from landing stages at Vigadó tér and Bem József tér

The Danube (Hungarian Duna) flows through Budapest from north to south; within the city boundaries its widest place 640 m (700 yds) is in the north of the city just below the junction of the two arms of the river which enclose the island of Szentendre (Szentendrei-sziget). The river is at its narrowest 283 m (310 yds) below Gellért Hill; here it is about 9 m (30 ft) deep.

Flooding

Until the late 19th century rises in the water level led to considerable insecurity in the districts near the Danube. Then the width of the river could exceed 1000 m (1100 yds), and in the lower lying parts of the city considerable damage could be caused. Therefore in the second half of the last century measures to regulate the flow of the water were urgently put in hand.

Waterway

With the expansion of industry in Budapest and in locations further upstream, the Danube became of increasing importance for the movement of goods, and in the preceeding century the capacity of the port installations of the island of Csepel (Csepel-sziget) – see entry – was considerably increased. Along the Danube Corso on the Pest bank landing stages for national

Industry on the Danube

Central Market Hall in Dimitrov tér

and international passenger ships were built and these were
heavily used.

The Danube is at present spanned by two railway bridges (the
New Pest Bridge and the South Rail Bridge) and by six road
bridges (Margaret Bridge, Petőfi Bridge, and – see entries –
Árpád Bridge, Chain Bridge, Elisabeth Bridge and Freedom
Bridge).

Bridges

---

*Danube Bend (or Danube Knee; Dunakanyar)

The Danube Bend between Esztergom and Szentendre (see
entries) is one of the most delightful scenic reaches of the
whole course of the river and is often referred to as the "Hungarian Wachau". Wildly romantic landscapes, remains of
Roman and medieval fortifications, venerable little towns and
magnificent views attract thousands of tourists every year.
Here the Danube breaks through the threshold of the Hungarian Central Uplands. On the right bank rise the foothills of the
Bakony Forest, notably the Pilis range (Pilis-hegység) which
reaches a height of 757 m (2480 ft). From the north the Börzsöny
Mountains (Börzsöny-hegység), up to 865 m (2839 ft), slope
down towards the river. The Danube now follows a channel
defined by structural movement in bends and a definite loop
near Visegrád (see entry); shortly before reaching Vác (see
entry) it divides into two arms (Island of Szentendre) and from
its previous west–east direction it now turns to the south (the
river's "knee").
Today the "Hungarian Wachau" and the hills which border it
are the favourite recreational area of Hungary after Lake Balaton. It is provided with areas of holiday homes, camp sites,
numerous inns and hotels.
See Esztergom
See Szentendre
See Vác
See Visegrád

Location
20–60 km (12–37 miles)
north and north-west of
Budapest

Route
Main road No. 11 Budapest–
Szentendre–Visegrád–
Esztergom
Main road No. 2
Budapest–Vác

Buses
From Engels tér, Budapest

Suburban Railway HEV
Budapest-Szentendre (from
Batthyány tér, Budapest)

Boat trips
From Vigadó tér, Budapest

Danube Corso (Dunakorzó)

D5(L4/5)

The bank of the Danube on the Pest side of the river between
the Chain Bridge and Elisabeth Bridge is locally known as the
"Danube Corso" (Dunakorzó). From here, especially in the evening when the lights are on, there is a fantastic view of the
Fishermen's Bastion, the Matthias Church, the Castle Palace,
the Gellért Monument, the Citadel and the Freedom Monument
on Gellért Hill.

Tram
2

Buses
2, 15

Deák Ferenc tér

See Inner Ring

Dimitrov tér

D/E6(M5/6)

Trams: 47, 49	The square at the Pest end of Freedom Bridge is named after Georgii Dimitroff, a Bulgarian pioneer of the Workers' Movement. In the square is a monument to Dimitroff by J. Kraschmaroff (1954), as well as a memorial to the fallen.
Trolleybus: 83	
Buses: 1, 9, 15	
Central Market Hall	On the south side of the square stands the Central Market Hall (Központi vásárcsarnok), built by Sam Petz in Neo-Gothic style. Near by is the Foodstuffs Exchange (completed in 1896) which has survived until the present, as the numerous foods (fruit and vegetables, spices, meat and sausage, pastry, fish, etc.) testify. Even arts and crafts, textiles (hand-embroidered blouses) and basketwork can be obtained here.
Karl Marx University	A short distance to the south can be found the Karl Marx University of Economic Science (Marx Károly Közgazdaságtudományi Egyetem). It is housed in the former Central Customs Office, built between 1870–1874 by Ybl in Neo-Renaissance style. The magnificent former Gala Court of the building, which is 170 m (558 ft) long, was converted into an assembly hall.

Disz tér

See Buda, Important Streets and Squares

Dominican Convent

See Margaret Island

Duna

See Danube

East Station (Keleti pályaudvar)

G5

Location VIII, Baross tér	The East Station is the largest and most important of the Budapest stations. Most of the international express trains which traverse Hungarian territory stop here.
Underground Station M2 (Baross tér)	The architecture of this main station is very fine; it was completed in 1884 to the plans of J. Feketeházy and G. Rochlitz and has been renovated several times since. The main façade in Neo-Renaissance style is adorned with two statues representing James Watt and George Stephenson.
Trams 23, 24, 36, 44, 67	
Trolleybus 73, 76, 78	Murals by K. Lotz and M. Than embellish the prestigious station hall.
Buses 7, 7A, 33, 73E, 80, 95	In the square outside the station stands a Gábor-Baross Memorial (A. Szécsi; 1898) in honour of the former Trade and Transport Minister.

*Elisabeth Bridge (Erzsébet-hid)

D6(L5)

Buses 5, 7, 7A, 8, 8A, 78	The modern Elisabeth Bridge replaces a predecessor built at the turn of the century which, for many years, was the largest

East Station

Elisabeth Bridge

arched bridge in the world and which was destroyed in the Second World War.

The modern suspension bridge, built between 1961 and 1964 to plans by Pál Sávoly, is 378 m (413 yd) long and 27·5 m (30 yd) wide. At the Pest end of the bridge stands the Inner City Parish Church (see entry). Remains of the Roman camp known as Castrum Contra Aquincum have also been uncovered here. There is a sculpture by György Zala of the earlier Queen Elisabeth, who was murdered in Geneva in 1898.

Emmerich Baths

See Tabán

Engels tér (Engels Square)   D5(L/M4)

Underground Station
M1, M2, M3 (Deák tér)

Buses
2, 4, 4A, 6, 9, 16

Almost 2 ha (5 acres) in extent Engels tér was once the site of a cemetery and is today the location of the long-distance bus station. In the centre of a lawn stands the Danubius Fountain, designed by Ybl in 1883 and originally set up on Kálvin tér. The figures on the fountain by L. Feszler were overhauled by D. Győri in 1959. They symbolise the Danube and its three largest tributaries, the Drau, the Theiss and the Save.

On the east side of the square is a marble memorial by G. Kiss (1906) commemorating Frau Veres (1815–95), who was outstanding in the field of education for women.

J. Horvay (1929) was the sculptor of the bronze figure of a shepherd playing a pipe, on the north-west side of the square.

Of considerable architectural merit are the buildings in the Classical manner at József Attila utca Nos. 1 and 2 and the building by J. Hild at József Attila utca No. 16.

Eötvös tér

See Roosevelt tér

Eötvös University

See Loránd-Eötvös University

Ernst Museum

See Nagymező utca

Erzsébet-hid

See Elisabeth Bridge

**Esztergom (Gran)

Information
Széchenyi tér

Esztergom (Gran) is one of the oldest towns in Hungary. It lies on the terraces of the right bank of the Danube at the place

where the river breaks through the Hungarian Central Uplands ("Hungarian Wachau"). The old residence of the Hungarian Princes and Kings has, since 1715, been the seat of the Catholic Prince Archbishop of Hungary.

Esztergom, which has many historic buildings, numbers today about 33,000 inhabitants. Since the end of the Second World War industry (especially engineering) has flourished to become, together with tourism, an important factor in the economy.

The Romans maintained a military camp on the site of the present-day town of Esztergom. From the end of the 10th c. the Hungarian Árpáds elevated Esztergom to the position of a Residence, where in 1189 the Hohenstaufen Emperor Frederick I, called Barbarossa, was welcomed. The burgeoning town was destroyed by Mongols in 1241 after which the Hungarian King transferred his residence to Buda. In 1526 after the Battle of Mohács, Esztergom became a frontier fortress of the Turkish kingdom, but in 1683 the Austrians reconquered the town. In 1715 the Residence of a Catholic Archbishop was made the seat of the Prince Archbishop of Hungary. From then on Esztergom had its heyday as a religious centre. The Cathedral of Esztergom, the largest and the most magnificent church in the whole of Hungary, was dedicated in 1856. In connection with this event Franz Liszt conducted his "Gran Festival Mass".

Location
60 km (37 miles) north-west of Budapest

Buses
From Engels tér

Boats
From landing-stage at Vigadó tér

History

Alsó-sziget (Danube Island)

The Island of Alsó-sziget, which is linked to the mainland by three bridges over the Kis-Duna, has in recent years been developed as a recreational park. Landing-stages, sports grounds, an open-air theatre and the very well-known inn, the Halász-csárda, provide for all kinds of leisure activity.

Location
between the Danube and the Kis-Duna

Old Church (City Parish Church; Öreg templom)

Built during the 1760s the so-called "Old Church" replaces a 13th c. Franciscan church which had been destroyed by the Turks. The reredos of the High Altar by the Hungarian painter János Vaszary (1867–1937) is exceptionally fine.

Location
Pór Antal tér

Bálint Balassi Museum (Balassi Bálint Múzeum)

This museum, named after Bálint Balassi, the Hungarian poet who fell in battle against the Turks near Esztergom in 1594, houses an interesting collection of archaeological and local historical material. The exhibits illustrate the history of Esztergom and include finds of the Middle Ages and of the Turkish era.

Location
Bajcsy-Zsilinszky út 63

Castle Hill (Vár-hegy)

The Castle Hill (156 m (512 ft)) is probably the oldest place of habitation within the boundaries of Esztergom. A few years ago

◀ *Esztergom*

Cathedral of Esztergom
Archiepiscopal
Cathedral Church
Főszékesegyház

1 Entrance Hall
2 North Tower
3 South Tower
4 St Stephen's Chapel
5 Bakócz Chapel
6 Treasury
7 Meeting Hall

Dome

50 m
55 yd

traces of Roman settlements were uncovered here. Also to be seen are the remains of the medieval king's castle and some ruins of the fortifications of the 14th and 15th c. The cathedral, surrounded by the former houses of the canons and the archiepiscopal seminary, is visible far and wide.

*Cathedral (Főszékesegyház)

Location
Szent István tér (Vár-hegy)

Esztergom Cathedral was begun in 1822. Its bold architecture, modelled on the Italian Renaissance, is the work of Paul Kühnel and J. B. Packh. The church was completed in 1856 by J. Hild. During the celebrations of the dedication festival Franz Liszt conducted his "Gran Festival Mass" which had been specially composed for the occasion.

Exterior

The exterior of the cathedral is of monumental proportions. The ecclesiastical building is 118 m (387 ft) long and its west front is 48 m (156 ft) wide. Over the crossing rises a dome, 72 m (236 ft) high, borne on twenty-four pillars (a winding staircase with 408 steps leads to the top). Two towers flank the entrance hall which is reminiscent of a Greek temple.

Bakócz Chapel

The most charming part of the interior is the Bakócz Chapel (Bakócz-kápolna), a reconstruction of a chapel commissioned in the first half of the 16th c. by Archbishop and Papal Candidate T. Bakócz. The altar created by A. Ferrucci of Florence is most striking.

Treasury

Numerous exceptionally valuable works of art are kept in the Cathedral Treasury. Of immeasurable value are a Byzantine tablet of the 11th c, a 12th c. Hungarian coronation cross, the "Hill of Calvary" by Matthias Corvinus dating from the 15th c. and various chalices and priestly vestments.

Crypt

In the crypt the magnificently carved tombs of the Archbishops of Esztergom are well worth seeing.

*Archbishop's Palace (Primási palota)

Location
Berényi Zsigmond u.

The Palace of the Primate of Hungary was completed in 1882 by the great architect Lippert, in Eclectic style. It contains sacred art brought together by Archbishop J. Simor. Carpets, tapestries and porcelain are also on view, as are works by Italian masters of the 12th to 15th c., among them examples by Lorenzo di Credi, Duccio and Lorenzetti, Hungarian panels, including a "Way of Sorrows" of the first half of the 16th c., an altar and a man's coffin from Garamszentbenedek, both of the 15th c.

Opening times
Daily 9 a.m.–5 p.m.

Hotel Fürdő

The baths of Esztergom have been known since Roman days. Adjoining the modern Hotel Fürdő, an imposing Classical building, are thermal indoor and outdoor baths; they occupy the same site as a bath in the 12th c.

Location
Bajcsy-Zsilinszky út 14

*Royal Palace (Királyi palota)

The remains of the oldest Hungarian Royal Palace are situated on the southern promontory of the Castle Hill. They are reputed to have been erected under Grand Duke Géza in the 10th c.
On the south side of the present cathedral are the remains of St Adalbert's Church (11th/12th c.) with the Porta Speciosa (red marble).

Location
Vár-hegy

Opening times
Daily 9 a.m.–4.30 p.m.

Passing through a long lapidarium (with some Byzantine capitals) one reaches a 12th c. tower dwelling. From the room in which it was reputed King Stephen was born (with red marble pillars in the centre) one first reaches the widow's quarters of Queen Beatrix, the consort of King Matthias, and then the Hall of Cardinal Virtues with beautiful frescoes of the school of F. Lippi.

Tower Dwelling

Hall of Cardinal Virtues

The 12th c. Castle Chapel is very impressive; it has a beautiful rose-window above the stepped doorway where a figure of St Anna can be seen. The interior contains fragments of medieval frescoes. On the left is a side chapel probably once the private chapel of the king or of the archbishop.

Castle Chapel

Around the remains of the old castle are the ruins of 14th and 15th c. military installations, such as the Leopold Bastion (lipót-bástya) on the south side and the castle gate (várkapu: with a drinking-water system) on the Danube side.

Military installations

Mihály Babits Museum (Babits Mihály Múzeum)

On the Elő-hegy which rises to the east of the town can be found the house of Mihály Babits (1883–1941), an author who was much read before the Second World War. The house is now furnished as a memorial to him.

Location
Elő-hegy

St Anne's Church (Szent Anna-templom; Kerek templom = round church)

St Anne's Church was built in the first quarter of the 19th c. to plans by Johann Baptist Packh. The artist had in his mind the great model of the Roman Pantheon. His church served as a model for the new Cathedral of Esztergom.

Location
Hősök tere

Esztergom

Castle Hill
Vár-hegy

Cathedral
(see plan)

Outline of the
medieval Church
of St Adalbert

Casemates

Gate tower

**Royal Palace
Királyi palota**

Leopold's
Bastion

```
50 m
55 yd
```

1 Entrance Terrace

2 Castle Chapel

3 Side chapels

4 János-Vitéz Hall

5 St Stephen's Hall

St Thomas's Hill (Szent Tamás-hegy)

Location
East towards the district of
Viziváros

From St Thomas's Hill, the second noticeable height of the town, there is a fine view of Esztergom and the Danube.
On the hill stands a chapel dating from 1823. It contains a notable "Way of the Cross" with 18th c. statues.

*Széchenyi tér

Location
In the district of Belvaros

One of the finest squares in the town is Széchenyi tér which is surrounded by a number of impressive buildings.

On the south side of the square stands the Town Hall (Városi tanácsház) which was completed in 1770. House No. 3 (pretty coat of arms) reveals the influence of the Romantic period; it was completed in 1862. House No. 7 shows Baroque and Rococo features. The architecture of houses Nos. 24 and 25 is in the manner of the second half of the 18th c. (this was known as "pigtail" style from the fashion of the time when men wore pigtails).

*Ethnographical Museum (Néprajzi Múzeum)   D4(L3)

The Ethnographical Museum is housed in the former Palace of Justice, which had been built in 1896 in Neo-Renaissance style according to the designs of A. Hauszmann.

Over the tympanum, which is borne on six tall columns, can be seen a troika with the Goddess of Justice by K. Senyei. In the entrance hall are wonderful frescoes by K. Lotz.

The museum, which was opened in 1872, is primarily devoted to a collection of Hungarian cultural assets. Part of the extensive Hungarian collection is on show on the first floor. Here articles of rural life, implements for handwork and craft, unusual examples of handicraft and textiles can be seen. Special exhibits are concerned with ethnic groups from Central Asia and Siberia who are related to the Magyars, at least as far as their language is concerned.

On the second floor all the important levels of civilisation and their development are made clear. Of special interest are the New Guinea collection of L. Biró and S. Fenichel, the African collection of S. Teleki and E. Torday and evidence of the culture

Location
V, Kossuth Lajos tér 12

Underground Station
M2 (Kossuth tér)

Tram
2

Trolleybuses
70, 78

Opening times
Tues.–Sun. 10 a.m.–6 p.m.

Folk Music
Sun. 11 a.m. (Grand Hall)

Ethnographical Museum

Parizsi udvar in Felszabadulás tér

of the New Stone Age in Central Asia, Siberia, Mongolia, Africa, South America and the Pacific.

Europark

See Buda, Important Streets and Squares, Bécsi kapu tér

Evangelical Church

See Inner Ring, Deák Ferenc tér

Evangelical National Museum

See Inner Ring, Deák Ferenc tér

*Felszabadulás tér (Liberation Square)   D5(M5)

Location
District V

Underground Station
M3 (Felszabadulás tér)

Buses
7, 7A, 8, 8A, 15, 78, 112

Felszabadulás tér, the busiest square on the southern part of Pest's "shopping centre", has several architectural styles and is one of the most charming squares in the town.
On the side which faces the Danube (see entry) and on both sides of the Szabadsajtó út are two buildings protected by towers, the Klothild Palace and the Mathild Palace, built by K. Giergl and F. Korb in 1902 in Eclectic style. The Belvárosi Lido café has recently been installed in the Klothild Palace; a programme of folk-lore is held here in the early afternoon, followed later by performances of coffee-house music and jazz. In the evening there is a programme of international revue, with a variety show after midnight.

Párizsi udvar

On the north-west side of the square at the beginning of Kigyó u., which forms part of the recently created pedestrian precinct of Pest, stands the Párizsi udvar, built in the most beautiful Art Nouveau style with elements of Italian and Turkish architecture. At the eastern tip of this complex of buildings, the headquarters of the National Travel Bureau IBUSZ can be found.

See Franciscan Church

*Ferenc-Hopp Museum of East Asian Art   F4
(Hopp Ferenc Kelet-ázsiai Művészeti Múzeum)

Location
VI, Népköztársaság útja 103

Underground Station
M1 (Kodály körönd)

Buses
1, 4

Opening times
Tues.–Sun. 10 a.m.–6 p.m.

The museum occupies the house of its founder F. Hopp (1833–1919). The collection comprises Japanese, Korean and Indian *objets d'art* (the majority dating from the 16th and 17th c.), including lacquer and bronze work, pictures, carpets, porcelain, jewellery and book illustrations. There is also an archaeological collection.
In the museum garden can be seen selected sculptures from various regions in East and South Asia.
The museum's Chinese collection has been transferred to the China Museum (see entry).

Ferencvárosi Torna Club

See Népliget

Ferihegy Airport

See Facts and Figures, Transport
See Practical Information, Airport

Fire Brigade Museum

See Kőbánya

Fishermen's Bastion (Halászbástya)

C4/5(M7)

On Castle Hill, at the place where in the Middle Ages the fishermen had their defence installations, the Fishermen's Bastion
was built behind the Matthias Church (see entry), between 1895
and 1902. Its towers, colonnades and embrasures, which were
designed in Neo-Romanesque style by F. Schulek, were
recently renovated. From the bastion there is a magnificent
panorama over the city.
In the south courtyard of the bastion stands a bronze equestrian statue of St Stephen (Szent István), the first King of Hun-

Location
On the north side of Castle Hill

Buses
16, 16A

Fishermen's Bastion

St Stephen

63

gary; it is a work of A. Stróbl, dated 1906. In the north courtyard are statues of the monks Julianus and Gellért by K. Antal (1937). From the bastion a double flight of steps leads down to the "watertown" (see Viziváros), past a bronze statue of St George. At the bottom of the steps a memorial to János-Hunyádi, made in bronze in 1905 by István Tóth, can be seen.

Florian Chapel

See Viziváros

Flórian tér

See Óbuda

Fortuna utca

See Buda, Important Streets and Squares

Foundry Museum

See Viziváros

*Franciscan Church (Ferenciek templom)   D5(M5)

Location
V, Felszabadulás tér

Underground Station
M3 (Felszabadulás tér)

Buses
5, 7, 7A, 8, 8A, 15, 78

The Franciscan Church dominates the north-west side of Felszabadulás tér. This church, which has recently been renovated, dates from the first half of the 18th c. It is built in Baroque style and is the successor to a church which Franciscan monks had founded on this site in the 13th c. In 1541 the Turks turned the church into a mosque.

The façade facing Felszabadulás tér (see entry) is adorned with statues of St Peter of Alcantara, St Francis and St Antony, as well as the arms of the Franciscan Order (over the doorway). On the north-west exterior wall (Kossuth Lajos utca) can be seen a bronze relief by Holló (1905) commemorating Baron Wesselényi, who saved numerous people from drowning in 1838 during a flood. The interior of this single-aisled church has a magnificent High Altar and richly furnished side altars. A special treasure is the wooden pulpit with the Twelve Apostles. On the walls are frescoes by K. Lotz (1895) and V. Tardos-Krenner (1927).

The artists J. Fessl and F. Uhrl (1835) were responsible for the pretty Naiad Fountain outside the church.

Franz Liszt Academy of Music   E4(N3)
(Liszt Ferenc Zeneművészeti Főiskola)

Location
VI, Liszt Ferenc tér

The Academy of Music established by Franz Liszt (see Notable Personalities) is housed in a prestigious building designed in

Secessionist style by the architects F. Korb and K. Giergl between 1904 and 1907. On the main façade is a bronze seated statue of Franz Liszt by A. Stróbl.

In the foyer is a bust of Bartók by A. Beck and a sculpture representing the composer Chopin.

The Grand Hall on the ground floor occupies two levels and has room for an audience of up to 1,200; it boasts exceptionally good acoustics. Fine reliefs in the corners of this hall are the work of the artists Groh and Telcs.

The small hall on the first floor is less elaborately furnished. In its foyer is a wall-painting by J. Zichy which symbolises some of the stages in the development of Hungarian music.

The Franz Liszt Academy of Music is now a cultural institution known far beyond the boundaries of Hungary. After Franz Liszt, such well-known musicians as Béla Bartók and Zoltán Kodály worked here (see Notable Personalities), as well as Ernő Dohnányi and Leo Weiner.

The Academy has probably the most important collection of Hungarian musical literature.

Underground Station
M1 (November 7 tér)

Trams
4, 6

Trolleybuses
70, 78

Buses
1, 4, 4A, 12, 12A

Freedom Bridge (Szabadság-híd)

D6(M5/6)

The steel Freedom Bridge, which links Gellért tér on the Buda bank of the Danube with Dimitrov tér on the Pest side, was opened to traffic in 1896. The plans were by J. Feketeházy. The bridge, which is 331 m (362 yd) long and 20 m (22 yd) wide was destroyed in the Second World War but was the first bridge to be rebuilt, and it was reopened to traffic in 1946.

Trams
47, 49

Buses
1, 9, 15

Freedom Square

See Szabadság tér

Gellért Hill (Gellért-hegy)

C/D6(K/L5/6)

Probably the most striking feature of the landscape of the Hungarian capital is the panoramic Gellért Hill (235 m (771 ft)): a block of dolomite, the east flank of which falls steeply down to the Danube, the west side consists of terraces which were formerly vineyards. Along its geological fault several medicinal springs emerge which supply the Gellért Baths, Rudas Baths (see Practical Information, Spa Establishments) and the Raizen Baths. The hill is named after Bishop Gellért (see Notable Personalities) who did good works during the time of King Stephen I. According to legend this monk died as a martyr in 1046 on Gellért Hill, which was once thought to be a meeting-place of witches.

Location
Districts I and XI

Bus
27

Tram
19

---

*Gellért Monument

D6(L5)

On the north-east slope of Gellért Hill stands a statue of the Bishop, the work of G. Jankovits (1902); it is framed by an imitation antique pillared portico. Below the memorial is a man-made waterfall.

Location
Near the Buda end of Elisabeth Bridge

Gellért Hill

View from Gellért Hill of the south of Budapest

Gellért Monument

Liberation Monument

*Liberation Monument

On the south-east point of Gellért Hill is the Liberation Monument, commemorating the victorious Soviet Army in the Second World War; it was designed by the artist Zsigmond Kisfaludy Stróbl (1947).

On the limestone plinth stands a female figure, 14 m (46 ft) high, bearing a palm branch. At the foot of the monument can be seen a bronze statue of a Soviet soldier with the Red Flag, flanked by the symbols of progress and destruction.

Location
The south-east point of the hill

Jubilee Park (Jubileumi Park)

C/D6(K/L6)

The Jubilee Park was laid out on the occasion of the ceremonies celebrating the fortieth anniversary of the October Revolution. Charming walks, flower-beds and valuable artistic sculptures, among them "Budapest" by István Kiss, attract many visitors on fine days.

Location
XI, the southern slope of Gellért Hill

Citadel

C/D6(L5)

The Citadel, built by the Austrians on the summit of Gellért Hill after 1851 is still in good repair. Parts of the fortifications, more than 200 m (220 yd) long and up to 60 m (65 yd) wide, are open to the public (hotel, folklore restaurant in the casemates, exhibitions and viewing platform).

Location
I, summit of Gellért Hill

**Gellért Hotel and Thermal Baths
(Hotel Gellért Gyögyszallo, Gellértfürdó)

D6(L/M6)

The famous medicinal baths and hotel complex (see Practical Information, Spa Establishments) is, after its recently completed renovation, one of the finest of its kind in Budapest.

There was a spa here as early as the 13th c., when the thermal waters of Gellért Hill were used for medicinal purposes. According to the chronicler Evliya Çelebi of Istanbul the Turks extended the establishment and converted it into a luxurious spa.

The plans for the hotel, which was built in Secessionist style between 1911 and 1918, were by A. Hegedüs, A. Sebestyén and J. Sterk; today it appears in a new light and many well-known people have stayed here. The therapeutic bathing and treatment facilities have been excellently renovated and modernised since 1983 (covered thermal bath, the roof of which can be opened, bubble bath, Turkish bath, etc.), together with open-air facilities including a thermal bath with wave-making equipment which has been designed according to the most modern technical ideas.

Location
1, Szent Gellért tér

Trams
9, 18, 19, 47, 49

Buses
1, 7, 7A, 86

Rudas Baths (Rudas-fürdó)

D6(L5)

At the foot of Gellért Hil, at the Buda end of Elisabeth Bridge, are the Rudas Baths (see Practical Information, Spa Establishments). The thermal springs here were already in use in the Middle Ages; the first bath-house dates from that period. In the 16th c. the Turks extended the installation. The typical domed building with its octagonal main room has been preserved from that time. As well as the steam (Turkish) bath there is a

Location
I, Döbrentei tér 9

Trams
9, 19

Buses
5, 7, 7A, 8, 8A, 78, 112

Gellért baths outdoors . . .   *and indoors*

pump-room, where medicinal water from the Juventus and Hungária Springs is available.

Gentlemen's Street

See Buda, Important Street and Squares, Úri utca

Geological Institute (Földtani Intézet)   G/H4

Location
XIV, Népstadion út 14

Trolleybus
77

The buildings of the Institute (1898–1900) in Secessionist style were the work of Ödön Lechner and are notable for their colourful ceramic decoration. On the roof can be seen a sculpture representing three men bearing the world. In front of the building is a monument by A. Stróbl to the geologist and former Director of the institute, J. Böckh. Inside is a highly interesting geological collection.

Golden Stag

See Tabán

Gorsium

Location
70 km/43 miles south-west of Budapest

Near the Tác motorway exit (M7) is the Gorsium open-air museum, where remains of a Roman settlement have been unearthed and partially reconstructed. This settlement (1st–

5th c. A.D.) was situated at an important road junction. The museum will give you an impression of how Roman places of worship, villas and baths once looked.
A lapidarium contains items that have been found, including pottery, glassware and bronzework.

Gran

See Esztergom

Greek Church

See Petőfi tér

Gresham Palace

See Roosevelt tér

Gül-Baba-Türbe

See Rose Hill

Halászbástya

See Fishermen's Bastion

*Heroes' Square (Hősök tere)   F3

The extensive Heroes' Square at the western edge of Városliget (see entry) forms the crossing-point of Népköztársaság útja and Dózsa György út. Its layout was chiefly the work of the architect Albert Schickedanz who was also largely responsible for the huge buildings of the Museum of Fine Art and the Art Gallery which flank the square.

Underground Station
M1 (Hősök tere)

Trolleybuses
75, 79

Buses
1, 4, 20, 30

The Millennium Monument (Milleniumi emlékmű) is the dominant feature of the square. The 36 m (118 ft) high column is crowned by a figure of the Archangel Gabriel by György Zala. Round the plinth can be seen a group of horsemen in bronze representing the conquering Prince Árpád and six of his fellow warriors. On either side of the column, colonnades extend in a half circle. Between the individual columns are statues of Hungarian regents. On the corner pillars are works in bronze by György Zala representing Work and Prosperity, Chariots of War, Yolk of Peace and Knowledge and Fame. In front of the Millennium Monument is a memorial to the Unknown Soldier.

Millennium Monument

The splendid building in Classical-Eclectic style, which was completed in 1895, serves as an exhibition gallery for various

Art Gallery
(Műcsarnok)

69

Millennium Memorial in Heroes' Square

artists. The architecture, which is embellished with colourful ceramic work, was originated by the great Albert Schickedanz. Round the building is an open-air art exhibition.

Museum of Arts and Crafts   See entry

Hess András tér

See Buda, Important Streets and Squares

Historical Museum

See Castle Palace

Hungarian Academy of Science

See Roosevelt tér

Hungarian National Gallery

See Castle Palace

Hungarian National Museum

See National Museum

Hungaroring

The Hungaroring was opened in 1986. In August every year important Formula 1 motor races are held on this ring road. In addition, motor cycle and trucking competitions take place, such as the "Truck Trophy". Technical details: total length 4014 m/4390 yd, maximum gradient 7%, longest straight 700 m/766 yd. There are 25,000 seats and 150,000 standing places for spectators.

Location
16 km/10 miles north-east of the city centre, near Mogyoród

Access
Via the M3

HUNGEXPO

See Kőbánya

---

*Imperial Baths and Luke's Baths
(Csásár-fürdő és Lukács-fürdő)

C3

---

*Imperial Baths (Csásár-fürdő)

C3

The Imperial Baths are one of the oldest of their kind in Budapest. They originated in a Turkish bathing establishment (Hamam) which was in existence under Sokollu Mustafa Pasa. The octagonal domed main room dates from that period and from 1806 Classical additions were made.

Adjoining the wing facing the Danube (see entry) is the Béla-Komjádi Sports Bath (Komjádi Béla Sportuszoda) which was

Location
II, Frankel Leó utca 31

Tram
17

Béla-Komjádi
Sports Bath

Imperial Baths

Luke's Baths

71

opened in 1976; this has room for 2,000 spectators, and in good weather the roof can be opened.

*Luke's Baths (Lukács-fürdő)   C3

Location
II, Frankel Leó utca

Tram
17

An open-air layout connects the Imperial Baths with Luke's Baths to the south. The latter establishment, which is no less renowned than the former, was extended many times from 1760 onwards. Its pump-room is visited daily by a great number of convalescent patients. Adjoining Luke's Baths is a spa treatment centre which is equally well attended.

Institute of Physiotherapy and Rheumatology

To the south of Luke's Baths is the world-famous Institute of Physiotherapy and Rheumatology (Reuma és Fizioterápiás Intézet).

Mill Pond

Opposite Luke's Baths lies the Mill Pond (Malom-tó), the water-level of which depends on the flow from the thermal springs in the vicinity. On its northern side is St Stephen's Chapel, designed by J. Hild (1844) which has a notable reredos.

---

*Inner City Parish Church (Belvárosi plébánia-templom)   D5(L/M5)

Location
V Március 15 tér/
Szabad Sajtó út

Trams
2, 2A

Buses
5, 7, 7A, 8, 78

History of the Building

The Inner City Parish Church is the oldest church in Pest (see entry). It stands on the remains of the Roman Castrum Contra Aquincum at the Pest end of Elisabeth Bridge (see entry).
In the 11th c. there was a little church here in which in 1046 Bishop Gellért (see Notable Personalities) was buried. In the 12th c. a semicircular choir was added. At that time the church was already being used by the Royal Family.

Extensive rebuilding in the Gothic manner according to French models took place under King Sigismund. The side chapels were added in the second half of the 15th c. During the Turkish occupation the church functioned as a mosque. On the south-west wall of the choir remains of a Turkish mihrab (niche showing the direction of Mecca) can still be seen. During the siege and the recovery of the neighbouring old royal town of Buda (see entry) by Austrian troops in the years 1684–86, the church was considerably damaged. Years later, rebuilding took place in Baroque style. In 1726 the church received its south tower, in 1735 its new nave and in 1739/40 the north tower. Restoration was undertaken in 1805–08 by J. Hild, and eighty-one years

Pest
Inner City
Parish Church
Belvárosi
plébánia-templom

1 Main Doorway	4 Triumphal Arch
2 North Tower	5 Chapel
3 South Tower	6 Former Mihrab

10 m
11 yd

later it was refashioned in Gothic style by the architect Emmerich Steindl. K. Lux worked on the church from 1932 to 1944. In 1948 work began on rebuilding the church which had been severely damaged in the Second World War.

The juxtaposition of two different styles is very impressive. Although the nave and towers have remained in Baroque style the choir reveals the Gothic influence. The main doorway has beautiful statues by Anton Hörger from Buda and on the external wall of the choir is a figure of St Florian also by Hörger.

Exterior

The side altar of John the Baptist (18th c.) is a jewel of art; it was the gift of Proberger, the Burgomaster of Pest. Also notable are the two Renaissance epitaphs in red and pale yellow marble and the pulpit constructed in 1808 by Ph. Ungnad. In the spandrels of the pointed arches in the polygonal south chapel the remains of frescoes can be seen. The modern High Altar was designed by Károly Antal and P. C. Molnár (1948). In the Baptistery is a bronze group by B. Ferenczy (1955).

Interior

*Inner Ring (Kiskörút)

D5–E6(L4–M/N5)

The Inner Ring (Bajcsy–Zsilinszky út–Deák Ferenc tér–Tanács körút–Múzeum körút–Kálvin tér–Tolbuhin körút) encircles the old town centre of Pest and follows the former town walls. In recent times Engels tér (see entry) has been included in the Inner Ring.

Locations
District V

Trams: 47, 49

Buses: 1, 9

Bajcsy–Zsilinszky út

D4/5(M3/4)

Bajcsy-Zsilinszky út is one of the finest streets in the Hungarian capital. Along it are many buildings in Romantic and Eclectic style.

See entry

Engels tér

Deák Ferenc tér

D5(M4)

Deák Ferenc tér which adjoins Engels tér (see entry) on the south-east is one of the most important inner-city traffic junctions. Three Underground lines meet here. Of special merit is the Evangelical Church (Evangélikus templom; Lutheran Church) which was built at the beginning of the 19th c. to plans by M. Pollack. The main façade was rebuilt by J. Hild in 1856. The altar is a copy of Raphael's "Transfiguration".

Underground Station
M1, M2, M3 (Deák tér)

At present the Evangelical National Museum (Evangélikus Országos Múzeum) is housed in the church and contains very interesting exhibits of church history. Near the church stands the minister's house and the former Evangelical secondary school, both fine Classical buildings.

Evangelical National Museum

The Underground Museum (Földalatti Vasúti Múzeum) occupies a tunnel dug in 1896 for the then first electric Underground railway in Europe. Interesting documents and exhibits, including technical objects, models, drawings, as well as some early carriages, illustrate the development of this mass transport undertaking which was so important for the Hungarian capital.

Underground Museum

Tanács körút (Councillors' Ring) — D/E5(M4)

Madách House — In recent years Tanács körút has become an important business street. On its north-east side stands the so-called Madách House (1937), a striking complex of buildings surrounding Madách Imre tér. This is the home of the Madách Studio Theatre. Opposite the Madách House is the exhibition hall of the City Council (No. 4).

Film Museum — In the Film Museum (Film Múzeum; No. 3) performances are given, chiefly of meritorious old films.

Múzeum körút (Museum Ring) — E5/6(M/N5)

Buildings — In the Museum Ring two leading Hungarian cultural institutions are located: the National Museum (Nos. 14–16; see entry) and the Neo-Renaissance buildings of the Faculty of Natural Science of Eötvös-Loránd University (see entry), which were designed by Emmerich Steindl. Also of architectural merit is No. 7 for which Ybl was responsible in 1852. In the courtyards of Nos. 17 and 21 remains of the city walls of Pest can still be seen.

National Museum — See entry

Kálvin tér (Calvin Square) — E6(N5)

Underground Station
M3 (Kálvin tér) — Kálvin tér, on the southern edge of the centre of Pest, was once known as Széna tér (Hay Market). Today it is an important traffic junction. A few years ago, during building work, remains of the former Kecskeméter Gate of the old city fortification of Pest were discovered here. There are some interesting buildings round the square, including the former inn, The Two Lions (No. 8) dating from 1818. A little aside to the east in Baross tér is the Ervin-Szabó Library (Szabó Ervin Könyvtár) in a 19th c. Neo-Baroque building by A. Meining.

Reformed Church — This single-aisled church in a severe Classical style was designed by J. Hofrichter between 1816 and 1859 and built with the co-operation of J. Hild. The four columns of its notable portico bear a tympanum. The interior has a good coffered ceiling and an organ-case designed by Hild. On the left-hand side wall is the funerary monument of Countess Zichy, with a statue by R. Gayard (1854). In the church treasury are valuable articles of goldsmiths' work dating from the 17th, 18th and 19th c.

Tolbuhin körút (Tolbuhin Ring) — E6(M5)

Tolbuhin körút has in recent years become a busy shopping street, due chiefly to the proximity of the Central Market Hall (see Dimitrov tér). One of the finest buildings in Tolbuhin Ring is No. 12, a fine example of the Classical style. There is a beautiful figure of a dancer in its courtyard.

Institute of Physiotherapy and Rheumatology

See Imperial Baths and Luke's Baths

Jewish Museum

See Pest Synagogue

*Joseph Town Parish Church (Józsefvárosi plébánia-templom)   F6

The imposing Joseph Town Parish Church with its twin towers
was built at the end of the 18th c. in Late Baroque style according to plans by J. Thalherr. Since then it has been altered on
several occasions. Fine examples of ecclesiastical art are the
High Altar by József Hild and the reredos, the "Apotheosis of St
Joseph" by the famous Viennese painter Leopold Kupelwieser.
On the façade, between the two towers, a statue of St Joseph
by L. Dunaiszky can be seen.
In front of the church stands a monument by Péter Pázmány
(see Notable Personalities) to the Bishop of Esztergom and
founder of the University of Tyrnau, the precursor of the University of Budapest.
On the other side of Baross útca lies Norváth Mihály tér, named
after the Catholic Bishop and Minister of Culture of 1849. His
memorial was the work of A. Domján in 1948.

Location
VIII, Baross útca/
Horváth Mihály tér

Trolleybus
83

Buses
9, 17

József Nádor tér (Archduke Joseph Square)   D5(L4)

The square commemorates Archduke Joseph of Habsburg
who was elected Palatine of Hungary (the King's deputy) in
1796 and who did a great deal for Budapest. Johann Halbig
created his monument in 1859.
The buildings round the square still retain something of the
atmosphere of the last century. This is especially true of No. 1
(1825), built by J. Hild, the outstanding representative of Hungarian Classicism, No. 5 (1859), which was designed according
to the ideas of the great Romantic architect H. Máltás, and No.
7, built in Classical style in 1833 by L. Zofahl. Near by stands the
very modern administration building of the Ministry of Finance
(Pénzügy-minisztérium).

Location
District V

Underground Station
M1 (Vörösmarty tér)

Bus
15

Jubilee Park

See Gellért Hill

Kálvin tér

See Inner Ring

Kapisztrán tér

See Buda, Important Streets and Squares

Kápolna

See Kőbánya

Karl Marx University

See Dimitrov tér

Károlyi Palace

See Petőfi Museum

Kerepesi Cemetery (Kerepesi temető; Pantheon Cemetery)   F–H5/6

Location
VIII, Mezo Imre út

Underground Station
M2 Keleti pál

Trams
23, 24, 29, 36, 37

Bus
33

The Kerepesi Cemetery is one of the largest in the Hungarian capital. Since the 1950s it has been a cemetery of honour in which notable people are buried.
The Munkásmozgalmi Pantheon (Pantheon of the Workers' Movement) is a monumental building erected by József Körner, with artistic details by Zoltán Kiss.
The mausoleums of Lajos Kossuth, Lajos Batthyány and Ferenc Deák (for all three see Notable Personalities) have places of honour; they were designed by Gerstl and Stróbl, Schickedanz and Gerstner respectively.

King's Bath

See Viziváros

Kiscelli Museum

See Obuda

Kiskörút

See Inner Ring

Kispest (Little Pest)   J/K8

Station
Kőbánya-Kispest

Underground Station
M3 (Kőbánya-Kispest)

Kispest has only existed since 1871 and is now part of District XIX. It is the headquarters of large industrial concerns, including the Red Star engineering works, the Ganz industrial combine and the Red October textile undertaking. Of particular interest from the town-planning point of view is the so-called "Wekerle Settlement" which was methodically laid out on a chess-board pattern between 1908 and 1925. It comprises more than 1000 dwellings.

Kőbánya   J/K6–8

Station
Kőbánya-felsó
Kőbánya-Kispest

Kőbánya (= quarry) forms District X of Budapest. Its name indicates that until late into the last century, building stone was quarried here. In the lengthy tunnels various beers are now stored and mushrooms grown.

In the centre of Kőbánya stands the Church of St Ladislaus (Szent László templon) which was built at the turn of the century from plans of Ödön Lechner. The architecture combines elements of Neo-Gothic and Secessionist styles. There is fine Zsolnay ceramic work on the altars and on the pulpit.

Trams
13, 28, 29, 36, 37

Buses
9, 17, 32, 51, 62, 85, 95, 117, 132, 168, 185

Rottenbill Park is named after a former Burgomaster of Pest. Zoltán O. Kiss created the impressive granite statue of Don Quixote.

Rottenbill Park

The Greek-Catholic Trinity Chapel (Kápolna) is one of the oldest buildings in Kőbánya. This Baroque church dates from about 1740 and has a very fine Baroque altar.

Kápolna

The Budapest Fire Brigade Museum (Tűzoltómúzeum) contains not only documents about the history of the fire brigade but also a collection of rare historic apparatus.

Fire Brigade Museum

HUNGEXPO

I–K5/6

The Budapest exhibition grounds are situated in the north of Kőbánya. International fairs are held here every year (May and September/October) and there is also a tourism exhibition (March) which is well attended. Every five years one of the largest agricultural shows of eastern Europe takes place here.

Tram
29

Bus
100

Kodály House

See Népköztársaság útja

Kodály körönd

See Népköztársaság útja

*Kossuth Lajos tér

D4(L3)

Kossuth Lajos tér is probably the most impressive square in the Hungarian capital. It is surrounded by monumental buildings. On the west side stands the Parliament Building and on the east side the Ethnographical Museum (see entries), the Ministry of Agriculture and Food (Mezőgazdasági és Elemezésügyi Minisztérium; 1885; architect: G. Bukovics) which is in Neo-Classical style. In front of this last-named building are two figures by A. Somogyi.

Location
District V

Underground Station
M2 (Kossuth tér)

Tram
2

Trolleybuses
70, 78

The south side of Kossuth Lajos is bordered by the Hungarian Chamber of Trade, which dates from 1972.

On the northern lawns of the square is a monument commemorating Lajos Kossuth (see Notable Personalities) by Zsigmond Kisfaludy Stróbl (1952); on the southern lawn is an equestrian statue of Count Ferenc Rákóczi II by János Pásztor (1935).

Kossuth memorial

Kossuth Monument

Ministries

Near Kossuth Lajos tér can be seen the Ministry of External Trade (Külkereskedelmi Minisztérium; Honvéd utca 13–15) and the Ministry of Defence (Honvédelmi Minisztérium, Honvéd utca 26–30). The last-named ministry is housed in a Classical building designed by J. Hild (1839); formerly this building was occupied by the most important silk factory in Pest.

Kossuth Lajos utca   D/E5(M4/5)

Location
District V

Buses
7, 7A, 78

Kossuth Lajos utca, one of the busiest streets in the Hungarian metropolis leads from Felszabadulás tér (see entry) to the Inner Ring (see entry). On both sides are shops, stores and inns.
At the north-east end of the street (near the Hotel Astoria) the medieval Hatvan town gate which was originally protected by a bastion stood, until well into the 18th c.

Kun Béla tér

See Üllői út

**Lake Balaton

Location
95–190 km (59–118 miles)
south west of Budapest

Lake Balaton (105 m (345 ft) above sea-level), which together with the surrounding area is the most important tourist region in Hungary, attracts more than 600,000 holiday-makers from far and wide every year. The high season lasts from July to September. The lake, which extends from south-west to north-east is 78 km (45 miles) long and up to 14 km (9 miles) wide. It was formed at the end of the Pleistocene period by tectonic sinking of the land. The lake is fed principally by the River Zala and the karst springs in the vicinity of Tapolca. The "Hungarian Sea", as it is called, occupies an area of over 591 sq. km (228 sq. miles) and is, therefore, the largest lake of central Europe. However, twice in the course of its existence it has dried up, owing to its relatively shallow depth (average 3–4 m (10–13 ft); deepest place 12 m (39 ft)) and the corresponding relatively small amount of water that it contains (about 1·8 billion cu. m (2·4 billion cu. yd).

The shallow Lake Balaton, which has frozen over on several occasions in winter, quickly warms up in summer. The surface temperature can reach 28 °C (82 °F). This and the configuration of the banks – the south bank is very flat and sandy, the north bank more sloping and with pretty bays – provide the best conditions for bathing and water-sports.

The north bank of the lake, the landscape of which is characterised by the foothills of the Bakony range and by evidence of volcanic action in the Pliocene Age, is everywhere delightful and is often called "the Hungarian Riviera". In the south-west, where the Zala joins Lake Balaton, lies Little Balaton (Kis-Balaton), an area which was originally boggy but the greater part of which has now been drained, with many rare plants and animals (especially birds) to be seen.

Access
By rail from Budapest Déli pu
(South Station)
By car from Budapest via
Motorway M 7 (E 96)

Buses
From Engels tér

General

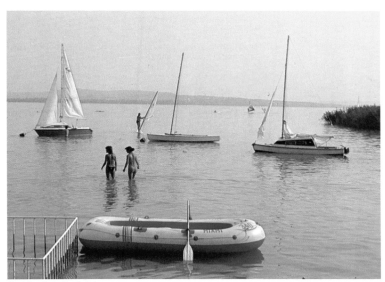

Bathing in Lake Balaton

Lake Balaton

North Bank (sights in alphabetical order)

Abrahám-hegy (Abraham's Hill)	Abraham's Hill is, with Badacsony the most celebrated vineyard on Lake Balaton. Monastery ruins.
Alsóörs	Alsóörs is in a charming situation on a terrace on the shore of the lake. Little harbour. Bathing beach. Above the village is the viewpoint Szabadság (296 m (971 ft)).
Badacsony	Well known for its wines, Badacsony (438 m (1438 ft)) is a hill which bears evidence of volcanic action in the Pliocene era. From it fine views may be enjoyed. There are imposing columns of basalt on the summit and slopes. Vines have been grown here for about 2000 years. Sándor-Kisfaludy House (1772–1844, writer), József-Egry studio (1883–1951, the "painter of Balaton"). There are popular wine festivals in Badacsony and district in autumn.
Balatonalmádi	Balatonalmádi is a resort at the north-east tip of the lake with one of the largest bathing beaches.
Balatonfüred	Balatonfüred, now a much-frequented holiday and spa centre, is the oldest resort on Lake Balaton. It has an establishment treating heart conditions (carbonic acid mineral spring; see Practical Information, Spa Establishments). First Hungarian yacht harbour. Pump-room. Attractive lake promenade. Mór-Jókai Museum. Beautiful walks. Course for water-skiing with a towing cable 1200 m (1313 yd) long.
Balatonfűzfő	Balatonfűzfő is an industrial town, as well as a tourist resort.
Balatongyörök	Balatongyörök lies on the southern declivity of the Keszthelyihegység. There are wildly romantic rocks and grottoes in the vicinity. A popular wine cellar.
Balatonkenese	Balatonkenese, an ancient settlement on the east bank of Lake Balaton has a church dating from 1606. At the north-west edge of the village can be seen loess caves which were once inhabited. Modern recreational centre by the lake.
Balatonrendes	Balatonrendes is known for its wine. Bathing beach; Bajcsy-Zsilinszky House.
Balatonszepezd	From the resort of Balatonszepezd there are opportunities for pleasant walks. Gothic church (13th c.).
Balatonudvari	There was a settlement here in Roman times. There are interesting tombstones (in the form of a heart) in the churchyard. Near by is the holiday estate of Kilián-telep.
Csobánc	The volcanic hill of Csobánc (376 m (1234 ft); basalt summit) lies at the end of the Tapolca Basin. Ruined 13th c. castle. At the south-west foot of the mountain is the "Rossztemplom, a subterranean church built in the 13th c.
Csopak	Csopak is a romantic vine-growing village. Ranold Castle and the Church of Kövesd are worth seeing.
Dörgicse	There is a medieval look to Dörgicse which is in a beautiful situation. From Halom-hegy (399 m (1310 ft)) there are magnificent views.

Of interest here is the Romanesque Protestant church dating from the 13th c.

Felsöörs

In the vicinity of the resort of Gyenesdiás are wine cellars full of atmosphere. Ilona Chapel. Starting-point for expeditions in the Keszthelyi-hegység.

Gyenesdiás

The health resort of Héviz (see Practical Information, Spa Establishments), 6 km (4 miles) west of Lake Balaton, has become known for its thermal lake which probably was formed during the last Ice Age. The temperature of the water, which has a sulphur content, ranges between 26–37 °C/79–98 °F; the area extends over 47,500 sq. m (5681 sq yd); the water produced amounts to 30,000 lt (6600 gal.) per minute; the mud at the bottom is slightly radioactive. There are numerous medical and convalescent homes. Beautiful promenades and walks and a casino.

Héviz

From 1739 Keszthely has been the residence of the Festetics (imposing Baroque castle) and birthplace of the composer Karoly Goldmark. It lies on the west bank of Lake Balaton and is a popular excursion venue. The Georgikon (1797), the first agricultural school in Europe, was the forerunner of the modern high school for agrarian science. Helikon Library, Balaton Museum, Gothic church 14th c.). In summer the Helikon Festival in the park of the Baroque castle. Near the town are the remains of the Roman settlement of Valcum and of Zalavár the ducal seat of the Slavs.

Keszthely

Nagyvázsony has become known because of the 15th c. Kinizsi Castle which was once an important frontier fortress. Open-air

Nagyvázsony

Héviz, lake fed by hot springs

Lake Balaton

ethnographical museum; monastery; Pauline monastery; in summer equestrian games.

Szent György-hegy

Szent György-hegy (414 m (1359 ft)) provides probably the most impressive evidence of Pliocene volcanic activity in the area of Lake Balaton. On the southern slope its basaltic covering is split into columns 30–40 m (100–130 ft) high. Excellent vineyards. Many wine cellars.

Sziliget

Of interest here are the remains of a 13th c. castle and the Avasi Church of the same period, as well as the former Puthéani Castle (18th c. Baroque), once owned by the Eszterhazy family. Bathing beach.

Tapolca

The thriving industrial town of Tapolca (10 km (6 miles) north of the lake; bauxite workings in the vicinity) was once well known for its wine trade. A grotto with a pool is popular; this is part of an extensive system of karst caves.

Tihany

The peninsula of Tihany is the most beautiful holiday resort on Lake Balaton. Luxurious hotels, a new holiday club, a marina (80 berths), places of recreation well equipped by the State, and other charming holiday homes give Tihany something of an exclusive character. In addition to the Biological Research Institute of the Hungarian Academy of Science and a branch of the Geophysical Institute, two other important research establishments are located in Tihany.

The only car-ferry across Lake Balaton plies between Tihany and Szantod on the southern shore.

The Tihany Peninsula, the higher parts of which are covered with basalt tufa, was the scene of volcanic activity in Late Tertiary and Quarternary times. It was then that a number of geysers broke through the hard tufa and formed the so-called "geyser humps". Later the central part of the peninsula sank and in the deepest place a sheet of water appeared, not unlike a crater lake. There are traces of a fortification, known as an "ovar", dating from early historical times, and this was later also utilised by the Slavs. Nothing is left of a fortification built after the attacks by the Mongols.

In 1055 King Andrew (Endre) I built the Benedictine Abbey of Tihany which now attracts many visitors. This religious foundation was extended in the 18th c. (monastery buildings and a beautiful Baroque church). Only the crypt of the original abbey church remains today.

Lake Balaton

The whole of Tihany is now a protected area. Part of it has been set up as an open-air ethnographical museum. In the vicinity are sweet-smelling lavender fields.

Zánka   Zánka is the largest vacation centre on Lake Balaton.

Zalaszántó   Zalaszántó has been inhabited for a very long time (finds of the Ice Age); it is situated on the northern side of Keszthely-hegység. The 13th c. church and castle ruins of the same date are worth seeing.

South Bank (sights in alphabetical order)

Balatonberény   In the old village of Balatonberény well-preserved and architecturally interesting old farmhouses and the 17th c. Fortress of Csillagvár are to be seen.

Balatonboglár   Balatonboglár is one of the oldest holiday resorts on the south shore of Lake Balaton. Near the little village of Buzsák, which is noted for its folk-art (especially costumes), the ruins of the 11th c. Benedictine Abbey of Somogyvár can be seen.

Balatonfenyves   From the resort of Balatonfenyves a narrow-gauge railway runs to Csiszta-puszta (medicinal baths).

Balatonföldvár   Balatonföldvár can look back on a long tradition as a summer resort. Extensive bathing beach; near by in Zala the house of Mihály Zichy (1827–1906) the Court Painter of the Russian Tsarist family.

Balatonlelle   Balatonlelle is very popular as an elegant holiday resort.

Balatonszárszó   In Balatonszárszó, a rather quiet resort, the Attila-József Museum is worth seeing. The poet died here. A 13th c. church.

Balatonszemes   Balatonszemes is growing quickly. The 15th c. church with a valuable reredos, the postal museum (documents, old wagons) and the "Owl Castle" (Bagolyvár) are among the attractions.

Fonyód   Fonyód, the second largest resort on the southern shore of Lake Balaton, extends along the foot of Vár-hegy (233 m (765 ft)), which was inhabited in prehistoric times. There are a harbour and remains of a medieval castle.

Siófok   Siófok, the largest place and the regional centre of the southern part of the area of Lake Balaton, has developed in recent years to become the most popular holiday resort on the lake. The increase in tourism is largely due to the building of the railway from Budapest to Fiume. The first baths were opened here in 1866.

Siófok, lies on the little River Sió, a fact which led the Romans to construct a canal here. It is the birthplace of the operetta composer Emmerich Kálmán. The Turks, who had established themselves in a 16th c. moated castle, controlled from here the entire area to the south of the lake. In 1863 the Sió Canal was extended at considerable cost.

There is a great deal of information on regional history to be found in the József-Beszédes Museum (history of the town, boating on Lake Balaton, building of the Sió Canal, an Emmerich Kálmán room).

Near Siófok are the remains of the Roman settlement of Tricciana.

Szántód is the terminus of the ferry to Tihany. Ferry-house and farmhouse (agricultural museum with 18th and 19th c. implements).

Szántód

The holiday resort of Zamárdi lies on the triangular spit on the south side of Lake Balaton.

Zamárdi

Lake Velence

Lake Velence has a slight salt content and covers an area of 25·3 sq. km (10 sq. miles). It is charmingly situated on a flat plain at the south-east foot of the Vértes mountain range. The lake is surrounded by a rich variety of flora and fauna. Many rare birds nest in the thick reed-beds.

Over the years the lake, with an average depth of only 1·5 m (6½ ft) and a water temperature as high as 25 °C (77 °F) in summer, has developed into a very popular spot for excursions. Increasing demands have been met by the provision of harbours for rowing-boats and small sailing-boats, as well as bathing beaches near Agárd and special quiet spots for those wishing to relax or fish.

Location
40 km (25 miles) south-west of Budapest

Léanyfalu

See Szentendre

Lenin körút

See Outer Ring

Liberation Monument

See Gellért Hill

Liberation Square

See Felszabadulás tér

Loránd-Eötvös University
(Eötvös Loránd Tudományegyetem)

D/E6(M5)

The central buildings of the Loránd-Eötvös University were erected at the end of the 19th c. in Neo-Baroque style to plans by Herczeg and Baumgarten. As well as the administrative headquarters of this university, which was founded in 1635 by Archbishop Péter Pázmány of Esztergom originally in Tyrnau, the buildings also house the faculty of law and political science.

Location
V, Egyetem tér 1–3

Underground Station
M2 (Astoria)

85

Luke's Baths

See Imperial Baths and Luke's Baths

Madách Theatre

See Outer Ring, Lenin körút

Március 15 tér (Square of 15 March)   D5/6(L5)

Location
District V

Trams
2, 2A

Buses
2, 5, 7, 7A, 8, 15, 78, 112

Contra Aquincum

The Square at the Pest end of Elisabeth Bridge commemorates in its name the outbreak of the Revolution of 1848.
Here the Romans had set up their Castrum Contra Aquincum, an advanced defence base, the purpose of which was to guard the Danube crossing. The remains of this fortification and documents illustrating its history can be seen in the lower part of the square. I. Tar was the sculptor of the "Legionaries' Fountain" (figures representing Roman legionaries) which dates from 1970.

Matthias Cellar

On the south-west side of the square is the lively inn, Mátyás pince (Matthias Cellar).

Inner City Parish Church

See entry

**Margaret Island (Margit-sziget)   C/D1–3

Trams
4, 6

Bus
26

Margaret Island, barely 2·5 km (1·5 miles) long and up to 0·5 km (550 yd) wide, is undoubtedly the local recreation and recuperative centre for the people of Budapest. Thermal springs, feeding the medicinal and swimming-baths, space for sports and games, carefully tended gardens and paths, and not least the remains of buildings which play a significant part in the history of the town daily attract many visitors.

History

The Romans utilised the supply of thermal water in the north of the island in the Danube. In the 12th and 13th c. Premonstratensian and Franciscan monks and Dominican nuns built monasteries and a nunnery here. Even the Archbishop of Esztergom and the Order of St John of Jerusalem maintained establishments on the island. At the end of the 18th c. the Habsburg Archduke John, Palatine of Hungary, had the island landscaped. At the end of the 19th c. a thermal bath with a pump-room was built, but in the Second World War this was severely damaged. After the war a modern spa centre was established including the fashionable Hotel Thermál, opened in 1978.

Name of the Island

The island gets its name from the canonised Princess Margarete (1252–71), the daughter of the Hungarian King Béla IV; because of a vow made by her father she became a nun in the Dominican convent on the island.

*Union Monument

In the south of the island stands a metal sculpture by István Kiss (1972) in the form of a flower; it was unveiled on the occasion of

View of Margaret Island

Union Monument

. . . detail inside the "leaves"

the centenary of the union of Obuda, Buda and Pest. On the inside surface of the leaves are symbols depicting the modern history of Budapest.

Fountain

Near the Union Monument is a large fountain, the waters of which are illuminated on summer evenings.

Alfréd Hajós Sports Bath

The Alfréd Hajós Sports Bath (Hajos-Alfréd Sportuszoda) in the west of the island is named after the double Hungarian champion of the first Olympic Games in modern times (1896). It was constructed in 1930/31 and includes a covered pool, two open-air pools, a diving-pool and two pools for children.
A short distance south is the Pioneer Stadium (Uttörő-stadion).

Franciscan Church (ruins)

Only scant remains have survived of the Church of the Franciscan Monastery which was erected in the 13th/14th c.; these include part of the west side, part of the north wall and of the apse, as well as a fragment of the tower.

*Palatinus Baths

The comprehensive facilities of the Palatinus Baths (Palatinus Strandfürdő) cover an area of 7 ha (17 acres). A bath with artificial waves, together with various medicinal, swimming and children's pools are fed with thermal water and can accommodate up to 20,000 at any one time.
Opposite the Palatinus Baths can be found the pretty Rose Garden (Rózsakert) with a little open-air animal enclosure.

Artists' Promenade

Along the Artists' Promenade (Művészsétány) can be seen busts of celebrated Hungarian personalities of the art world.

Dominican Nunnery (ruins)

After flooding which occurred in 1838, remains were discovered of the Dominican nunnery which had decayed during the Turkish occupation. The most celebrated nun was Princess Margarete (see above), the daughter of King Béla IV. The convent church was built in the 13th c., rebuilt in the 14th and extended in the 15th. Traces of Romanesque and Gothic architecture have been detected.

Water-tower

Near by stands a 52 m (170 ft) high water-tower (1911) which has been well restored. Close by can be found an open-air theatre with room for an audience of 3500.

Premonstratensian Monastery

Part of the foundations of the 12th c. Premonstratensian monastery are still to be seen. The church of this foundation was rebuilt about fifty years ago in Romanesque style. In the tower hangs a bell, cast in the 15th c., which is one of the oldest in Hungary.

*Spa Hotel Thermál

This hotel, completed in 1978, is extremely modern and has become well known far beyond the borders of Hungary. It was designed by the architect G. Kéry and is equipped according to the most recent balneological ideas. Near the hotel can be found an artificial rock garden (sziklakert) with rare plants of much interest.

Musical Fountain

The so-called "Musical Fountain" in the north of the island is a copy of one built in 1820 in Tîrgu Mureş in Romania by the Siebenburg specialist P. Bodor. The water-driven mechanism was destroyed in the Second World War.

Market Hall

See Dimitrov tér, Central Market Hall

*Martinelli tér

Martinelli tér was still in use as a market-place in the last century, but today it has become a busy "turntable" for traffic in Pest.
Of architectural interest is the former Servit Church (Szerviták templom), built in the first half of the 18th c. and rebuilt in the 19th. Its Baroque interior is very fine.

Location
District V

Underground Station
M3 (Deák tér)

Buses: 2, 15

The Béla-Lajta House (Lajta Béla-ház; No. 5) dates from 1912 and has recently been made a protected monument. Particularly attractive features of that period are the "hyper-modern" glass façade and the pretty ceramic decoration.

Béla-Lajta House

Just north of Martinelli tér lies Biermann István tér with a beautiful Danaid Fountain by F. Sidló (1933).

Biermann István tér

Marx tér

See Outer Ring

Matthias Cellar

See Március 15 tér

**Matthias Church
(Mátyás-templom; Church of Our Lady, Coronation Church)

The Church of Our Lady in Buda is one of the principal sights of the Hungarian capital. It is the successor to a church built in the time of King Béla IV (13th c.), which was rebuilt on several occasions. Its polygon side aisles date from the 14th c. as does the south doorway with its magnificent relief in the tympanum of the "Death of Mary". Side chapels were added in the 15th c. and an Oratory for the Royal Family and a new south tower, which bears the arms of Matthias Corvinus, dated 1470 (the original which gives the church its name is now to be found in

Location
Szentháromsá tér

Bus
16

See photo p. 28

Matthias Church
(Church of Our Lady)
Mátyás-templom

1 Main Doorway

2 Baptistery

3 Loreto Chapel

4 Mary Door

5 Entrance to Church Museum

89

Matthias Church

the interior). In 1526 the church was destroyed by fire and fifteen years later was converted into a Mosque. After the Turks were driven out by the Austrians, the Jesuits made themselves responsible for the Church of Our Lady and a few years later it became the Coronation Church of the Hungarian kings. It was rebuilt in its present form between 1874 and 1896 by F. Schulek who adopted the Gothic style. At the end of the Second World War the church was severely damaged but was faithfully restored after years of work.

A facsimile of the coat of arms of King Matthias which bears a raven, can be seen on the tower which is 80 m (263 ft) high, square at the bottom but octagonal from the second storey.

The richly ornamented south-west front is flanked by the little Béla Tower and the tall Matthias Tower. Above the doorway in the tympanum is a relief by Lajos Lontai (1890) in coloured granite showing the Madonna with two angels. Above this can be seen a fine rose-window.

A jewel of the varied south side of the church is the Mary Doorway which adjoins the Matthias Tower and opens into a portico. The fine relief in the tympanum representing the Death of Mary was created in the 14th c. On either side of the entrance are statues of King Stephen I (the Holy) and King Ladislaus I.

Interior

The Interior of the Church of Our Lady in Buda is decorated with geometrical designs and plant ornamentation, reminiscent of the painting in a mosque. The stained glass, some of which illustrates legends of saints of the tribe of Árpád, was made in the last century to designs by B. Székely and K. Lotz. The design of the High Altar is by F. Schulek in the Neo-Gothic style.

Loreto Chapel

The Loreto Chapel is situated in the church tower. It has a black Baroque Madonna on the winged altar and the original of the arms of Matthias Corvinus, dating from the year 1470.

Baptistery

The Baptistery in the Béla Tower still has medieval pillars and capitals. K. Lotz painted the frescoes.

Ladislaus Chapel

The chapel on the north of the choir is dedicated to St Ladislaus. Beautiful frescoes by K. Lotz illustrate scenes from the legend of Ladislaus.

Chapel of the Holy Trinity

Behind a grill enclosing the Chapel of the Holy Trinity in the north aisle can be seen the sarcophagi of King Béla III and his wife; they were originally buried in the Cathedral at Székesfehérvár and were reinterred in the Matthias Church in 1848.

Emmerich Chapel

A reredos by Mihály Zichy (about 1890) adorns the chapel dedicated to St Emmerich.

Church Museum

The crypt, the Oratory of the Knights of St John, St Stephen's Chapel near the Sacristy, and the Royal Oratory now serve as the church museum. In the Royal Oratory, the standards which were raised at the Coronation of King Charles IV and Queen Zita on 30 December 1916 still hang. In the museum are reliquaries, chasubles and other ecclesiastical treasures, and a replica of the Hungarian royal crown.

Millennium Monument

See Heroes' Square

Mill Pond

See Imperial Baths and Luke's Baths

Moszkva tér (Moscow Square)   B4(K/L6)

The triangular Moszkva tér (Moscow Square) is one of the most important traffic hubs of the inner city. The square is dominated by the brick building topped with a crown, which houses the postal administration. The fan-like roof of the Underground station is also a prominent feature.

Location
District XII

Underground Station
M2 (Moszkva tér)

To the north-east is Széna tér (Hay Square) with the former shooting range, built in 1826, and remains of the medieval fortifications of the town.

Széna tér

Municipal Circus

See City Woodland Park

Municipal Council (Fővárosi Tanács)   D5(M4)

A Baroque building, which is now the home of the Municipal Council of Budapest (picture see p. 8), was built between 1716 and 1728 to designs of Anton Erhard Martinelli. Its first use was as a home for those wounded in the Austro-Turkish campaign. Above the gates of the main façade are two fine reliefs, commemorating the Emperor Charles IV (Hungarian King Karl III) and Prince Eugene of Savoy.
In the south entrance gateway (from Kossuth Lajos utca) can be seen a "Pallas Athene" by Adami (1785), which once adorned the fountain outside the Matthias Church (see entry).
At the south end of the complex a relief by M. Kovács (1949) commemorating the rebuilding after the Second World War can be seen.

Location
V, Városház utca 9–11

Underground Station
M1, M2, M3 (Deák tér)

Trams
47, 49

Buses
1, 4, 4A, 9

On the southern forecourt stands an aluminium monument by the artist B. Szabados in memory of the first Mayor of the newly formed City of Budapest in 1873.

Southern forecourt

The 19th c. building with three inner courtyards (Városház utca 7), near the City Hall, is now the seat of the District Council of Pest. Of particular architectural interest is the Classical wing, constructed to plans by Matthias Zitterbarth, Junior.
In the first courtyard, which is surrounded by arcades, memorial tablets can be seen which honour the freedom fighters of 1848/49 and the victims of the Uprising of 1956.

District Council of Pest

Municipal Farm

See Városmajor

*Museum of Applied Arts (Iparművészeti Múzeum)   E6(N6)

Location
IX, Ulloi ut 33–37

Underground Station
M3 (Ferenc körút)

Trams
4, 6

Buses
12, 12A, 182

The Budapest Museum of Applied Arts, one of the oldest of its kind in Europe, dates from 1872; it is housed in a three-storey building which was erected between 1893 and 1896 to the design of Ödön Lechner and Gyula Pártos. The building was extensively damaged during the Second World War and rebuilt in the 1950s. With its domed projecting range it is an outstanding example of Oriental-Hungarian Secessionist style. The red granite facing of the exterior (prepared in the Zsolnay porcelain factory of Pćs) and the ceramic work which beautifies the roofs and corners is particularly fine.
Opening times from Tuesday to Sunday, 10 a.m. to 6 p.m.

Furniture

The collection comprises: old Hungarian furnishings, 18th c. French furniture, musical instruments and models.

Textiles

Ecclesiastical vestments and costumes, valuable Coptic weaving (4th–7th c.), Anatolian carpets, Renaissance materials, Dutch Gobelin tapestries, French, Italian and Hungarian lace and various other hand-crafted articles.

Precious metal work

Goldsmith's work (15th–17th c.); articles of silver, bronze, copper and pewter; old Hungarian and Siebenburg jewellery (some of it enamelled); clocks.

Glass and ceramics

Herend porcelain, faience by Holic and Tata, Haban cutlery, ceramics from famous manufacturers.

Small handcrafted articles

Carved ivory, pearl ornaments, leatherwork, bookbinding, various fashion accessories.

**Museum of Fine Arts (Szépművészeti Múzeum)   F3

Location
XIV, Dózsa György u. 41, Hönsök tere

Underground Station
M1 (Hósök tere)

Trolleybuses
75, 79

Buses
1, 4, 20, 30

N.B. Some rooms are temporarily closed

The Budapest Museum of Fine Arts is one of the most important European art museums. Its collection of Italian masters of the Renaissance enjoys an international reputation.
The Neo-Classical monumental building was completed in 1906 to the designs of Albert Schickedanz and Fülöp Herzog. The portico is very impressive; its huge Corinthian columns bear a tympanum with a relief inspired by one on the gable of the Temple of Zeus in Olympia.
Opening times from Tuesday to Sunday, 10 a.m. to 6 p.m.

There are a number of outstanding works among the very many on display:

Egyptian Department
Mummies and decorated mummy cases, gravestones, statues and statuettes, the remains of a Temple of Ptolemy.

Room 1

Graeco-Roman Department
Items dating from the 1st, 2nd and 3rd c. B.C., among them gold and bronze work and terracotta.

Room 2

Works of art of the 4th and 5th c. B.C., including the bronze Grimani jug, vases and an Attic tomb relief.

Room 3

Etruscan, Roman and Greek exhibits of the 1st c. B.C., notably the figure of a dancer and a Tyche statue.

Museum of Fine Arts in Hősök tere

Works of art of the Roman era, including the representation of the victory of the Emperor Augustus at Actium and attractive small sculptures.

Room 4

Renaissance Hall
In the centre of the hall are fine Venetian fountain wreaths. There are wonderful frescoes of the 14th, 15th and 16th c. from various places in Italy.

Department of Modern Sculpture
Works by European artists, among them the "Round Dance" by R. Rossi, the "Seated Woman" by Trubetzkoi, the representation entitled "A Mother's Sorrows" by Meštrović and Hildebrand's "Autumn".

Room 1

Works by French artists, including Rodin's "Eternal Spring", "Bronze Age", etc., bronze sculpture by Maillol, Carpeaux's "Spring" and a "Portrait of a Woman" by Despiau.

Room 2

Graphic Collection
The graphic collection comprises about 10,000 drawings, and some 100,000 engravings. From time to time exhibitions, chosen from this comprehensive stock, are mounted; these deal with particular epochs and schools, or with the works of outstanding artists. The collection includes studies by Leonardo da Vinci as well as drawings by Rembrandt, Manet, Cézanne, Gainsborough and numerous other well-known artists.

Engravings
Examples by Dürer, Rembrandt, Goya and other renowned artists.

Museum of Fine Arts

Art of the 20th Century
In this collection the works most admired are by Hans Arp, Marc Chagall, György Kepes, Pablo Picasso, Victor Vasarély and Fritz Wotruba.

Old Masters

Room 1	Tuscan painting of the 13th and 14th c. (especially sacred subjects).
Room 2	Tuscan painting of the 14th and 15th c., including work by Giovanni da Ponte and Taddeo di Bartolo.
Room 3	Works of art of the 15th and 16th c. from central Italy, among them examples from the school of Giovanni Santis, as well as works by Domenico and Rodolfo Ghirlandaio.
Room 4	Works of the 14th, 15th and 16th c. from northern Italy, including paintings by Gentile Bellini and Michele Pannonio (an artist of Hungarian origin).
Room 5	North Italian masters of the 16th c., including pictures by Bassano, Giorgione, Sebastiano del Piombo and Veronese.
Room 6	Piedmontese and other North Italian painters of the 15th and 16th c.
Galleries 1, 2 and 3	Italian masters of the 15th, 16th and 17th c., including works by Carracci, Correggio, Francesco Francia, Filippino Lippi and Lorenzo Lotto.
Room 7	Various Italian masters of the 16th and 17th c.
Room 8	Representatives of Italian Baroque painting, among them Bernardo Bellotto, Bernardo Strozzi and Giovanni Battista Tiepolo.
Galleries 4 and 5	Italian Baroque painters including Tiepolo.
Room 9	Dutch masters of the 16th and 17th c., including works by Pieter Bruegel the Elder.
Galleries 6, 7 and 8	Various Dutch masters of the 16th and 17th c., including works by Hans Memling and Jan Bruegel the Elder.
Room 10	Dutch paintings of the 17th c., including Rembrandt's "Old Rabbi" and "The Angel appears to Saint Joseph".
Room 11	Dutch masters of the 17th c.
Galleries 9–17	Works by various Dutch masters of the 17th c., among them paintings by Franz Hals, Jan van Goyen and Ruysdael.
Room 12	Flemish masters of the 17th c., including paintings by Rubens and Van Dyck.
Room 13	Flemish masters of the 17th c. (various artists).
Room 14	Spanish and Portuguese masters of the 15th and 16th c.
Room 15	Spanish masters of the 16th c., including works by El Greco.
Room 16	Spanish masters of the 17th c., including works by Esteban, Murillo and de Ribera.
Room 17	Spanish masters of the 17th c., with works by Goya ("Girl with a Jug", "Portrait of Señora Bermudez", etc.) and Velázquez ("Farmers at Table").
Room 18	German masters of the 15th c., with Hans Holbein's "Death of Mary".
Room 19	Various German painters of the 15th and 16th c., including works by Lucas Cranach, Albrecht Dürer and Hans Baldung Grien.

German Baroque painters, including Jan Kupetzky.   Room 20

German and Austrian painters of the 18th c., among them   Room 21
works by Angelika Kauffmann and Franz Anzon Maulbertsch.

English masters of the 18th c., including works by   Room 22
Gainsborough, Hogarth and Reynolds.

French masters of the 17th and 18th c., among them paintings   Room 23
by Chardin, Lorrain and Poussin.

Art of the 19th century
Special attention should be paid here to works by Böcklin,
Corot, Courbet, Delacroix, Cézanne, Gauguin, Leibl, Manet,
Monet, Pissaro, Renoir, Toulouse-Lautrec and Waldmüller.

Old Sculptures
The majority of the exhibits in this department are works by
Italian artists. The *piece de resistance* of the whole collection is
the equestrian statue by Leonardo da Vinci in Room 8. Also
noteworthy are Baroque works of art, including those by Georg
Raphaël Donner and Johann Christoph Mader.

Museum of the Hungarian Workers' Movement

See Castle Palace

Museum of Military History

See Buda, Important Streets and Squares, Kapisztrán tér

Music Academy

See Franz Liszt Academy of Music

Museum of Eastern Asiatic Art

See Ferenc-Hopp Museum of Eastern Asiatic Art

Musical Fountain

See Margaret Island

Museum körút

See Inner Ring

Nagykörút

See Outer Ring

*Nagymező utca (Pest Broadway)   D/E4(M3)

Location
District VI

Trolleybuses
70, 78

Nagymező utca crosses Népköztársaság útja (see entry) near the State Opera (see entry) and for a long time has been known as the Pest Broadway. Its reputation is not only due to the various establishments for night-life, among them the Moulin Rouge (No. 15), but also for the number of theatres in this street. The most important of these are the Municipal Operetta Theatre (Fővárosi Operettszínház; No. 17), the Thália Theatre (Thália-színház; No. 22), the political cabaret Mikroszkóp (No. 24) and the Literary Theatre Miklós Radnóti (No. 11).

Ernst Museum

In the Ernst Museum (No. 8) temporary exhibitions on various fine arts subjects are mounted.

Nagytétény

Station
Nagytétény

Tram
41

Buses
3, 13, 14, 101, 103, 113

Nagytétény is the most southerly part of Budapest (District XXII) on the Buda side of the Danube and is largely an agricultural region. From the 2nd to the 5th c. a Roman military camp was in existence.

In Nagytétény, which was probably named after a Magyar leader, viticulture played a major role from early times but in the last few decades has been gradually losing its former importance.

*Castle Museum (Nagytétény Kastély-múzeum)

Location
Csókási Pál utca 9

Opening times
Tues.–Sun. 10 a.m.–6 p.m.

The most important point of interest in Nagytétény is the Baroque castle which now houses a branch of the Museum of Applied Arts. The great country house was built in the 18th c. and use was made of remains of 15th c. buildings. It was severely damaged during the Second World War and a few years ago was carefully restored and opened as a museum.

Exhibits

Of interest are finely constructed furniture from the 15th to 19th c. (predominantly of Hungarian and German origin), and a collection of stove tiles and stoves. In some of the rooms are valuable paintings, carpets, china and clocks, dating from the 18th and 19th c. In the castle stables interesting finds of the Roman Age can be seen.

National Gallery

See Castle Palace

National Library

See Castle Palace, Széchenyi National Library

*National Museum (Magyar Nemzeti Múzeum)   E6(N5)

Location
VIII, Múzeum körút 14–16

The National Museum, founded in 1802 by Count Ferenc Szé-chenyi and which includes among its exhibits the Hungarian

Façade of the Hungarian National Museum

Royal Regalia, is housed in a large Classical building erected in 1847 to the plans of M. Pollack. The portico of the building is very impressive with Corinthian pillars supporting a triangular gable which is adorned with allegorical figures. In front of the museum stands a monument to the famous Hungarian poet János Arany (1817–82), which was created by A. Stróbl in 1893. In the park-like museum garden other busts and monuments of notable personalities can be seen.

Opening times: Tuesday to Sunday, 10 a.m. to 6 p.m.

On the ground floor are many interesting objects dating from pre- and early-historical times as well as from the Roman epoch and the age of the migration of peoples.

Notable among the exhibits in the Department of Pre- and Early-History (rooms I and II) are finds from Vértesszőlős and Sümeg. The *pièce de résistance* of the Bronze Age collection (rooms III and IV) is the Pécel cart. Room V is devoted to the Iron Age. The Roman period comes to life in the entrance hall and in rooms VI and VII. The complete preserved floor mosaic of the 3rd c. B.C. which was found at Veszprém is extremely beautiful and is on show in the foyer of the National Museum. In addition hand-crafted articles (some of them in bronze) and military objects are worth attention. Room VIII houses a coin collection. In the vestibule can be seen valuable evidence from the time of the great migration of peoples, including jewellery of the Huns, a Carolingian sword and utensils of Slav tribes.

On the first floor the history of Hungary from the occupation by the Magyars until the year 1849 is depicted.

A specially guarded room houses the Crown of St Stephen which is so surrounded by legends. It comprises a frontal circlet

Underground Station
M3 (Kálvin tér)

Trams
47, 49

Buses
1, 9

Ground floor

First Floor

surmounted by crossed bands, and is decorated with precious stones and pearls. The enamelled pictures of saints with which it is embossed and the characteristically lopsided cross on the top are also very beautiful. Sceptre, orb and sword lie next to the crown. The coronation robe is of Byzantine silk embroidered in gold and decorated with pearls. (See also photo on p. 23.)

In room III the Renaissance Stallum from Nyíbátor can be seen, as well as Hungarian and Turkish weapons. Mementos of the freedom fight of Prince Ferenc Rákóczi II in the 18th century can be found in room IV, and works of art from the Baroque age as well as mementos of the peasant uprising of the 18th century in room V. Rooms VI and VII are devoted to the 18th and 19th c. and include material and documents of the Hungarian Jacobin movement as well as of the Revolution of 1848/49. In room VI can also be seen Beethoven's grand piano, which later belonged to Franz Liszt.

Second Floor

Exhibits from the Science Museum are presented on the second floor. The collections of geological items (fossils, minerals and stones) and zoological specimens.

---

*Népköztársaság útja

D–G3–5(M/N3/4)

(Street of the People's Republic; formerly Andrássy út)

Location
District VI

Underground Stations
M1 (Bajcsy-Zsilinszky út–Mexikói út)

Buses
1, 4, 4A

The Budapest boulevard Népköztársaság útja which is 2·3 m (1·4 miles) long, was laid out from 1872 and leads in a north-easterly direction from Engels tér (see entry) to Hősök tere (see Heroes' Square). Fine palaces, important cultural buildings (including the State Opera and the Ferenc-Hopp Museum; see entries) and fine old villas line this imposing thoroughfare which since 1896 has been followed by one of the oldest underground railway lines of Europe.

Postal Museum

The Museum of the Hungarian Post Office (Posta Múzeum; No. 3) is housed in an unusual palace, which was designed by C. Czigler in the 1880s. The stairwell is embellished by fine ceiling-paintings by K. Lotz. As well as interesting documents concerning the development of the Hungarian post-office system, the postal history collection has original technical apparatus including the telephone of the Hapsburg Emperor Franz Joseph I and a transmitter of 1919.

Népköztársaság útja passes the State Opera House (see entry), crosses Pest Broadway (see Nagymező utca) and passes between Jókai tér (monument by A. Stróbl) and the Liszt Ferenc tér with the Franz Liszt Music Academy (see entry).

November 7 tér

The first section of Népköztársaság útja with its many Neo-Renaissance buildings ends at the octagonal November 7 tér. Here it crosses the Outer Ring (see entry) and continues as a boulevard on to Kodály körönd. In this stretch the following buildings are worthy of note: the former Academy of Music (No. 67) by A. Lang in Neo-Renaissance style, dating from 1879. This was also the home of Franz Liszt (memorial tablet).

Puppet Theatre

The State Puppet Theatre (Allami Bábszínház; No. 69) was also built by A. Lang in 1877. On its upper floor are frescoes by K. Lotz. L. Rauscher was the architect in 1875 of the Academy of Fine Art (Kepző muvészeti Foiskola; No. 71) in Neo-Renaissance style.

The Kodály körönd, a beautifully laid-out circular open space is named after the great Hungarian composer (see Notable Personalities). This square is bounded by statues of Hungarian freedom fighters: Vak Bottyán (d. 1709), by G. Kiss Kovács (1958); Miklós Zrínyi (d. 1566), by J. Róna (1902); György Szondi (d. 1552), by L. Marton (1958); and Bálint Balassi (d. 1594) by P. Pátzay (1959).

Kodály körönd

In the last section of Népköztársaság útja can be found at No. 89 the former residence of Zoltan Kodály and a palace (Nos. 88–90), dating from 1882, designed by G. Pertschacher with Neo-Renaissance work on the façade by L. Rauscher and a wrought-iron gate by G. Jungfer.

Kodály House

See entry

Ferenc-Hopp Museum of Eastern Asiatic Art

See entry

State Opera

*Népliget (People's Park)

H/I6/7

With an area of 112 ha (277 acres), Népliget is the largest park in the Hungarian capital. It was laid out in the 1860s to the southeast of the city centre. On the occasion of the centenary of the union of Obuda, Buda and Pest, Népliget was refurbished according to the latest horticultural ideas. The park with its various monuments, fountains and cascades, flower-beds, greenswards and old stands of timber, is extremely popular. In the north part of the park there is a motor-cycle race-track.

Location
District X

Underground Station
M3 (Népliget)

Tram: 23

Trolleybus: 75

Buses: 9, 17, 55

The Planetárium, opened in 1977 in the south-west part of Népliget, is one of the most modern of its kind in eastern Europe. In the dome-room (diameter 23 m (75 ft)) visitors can see an astro-show made possible by the use of Zeiss-Jena projection apparatus.

Planetárium

In the north-east corner of Népliget and outside the park to the south-west – on the far side of Üllöi út – lies the extensive sports ground of the historic Ferencvárosi Torna Club (FTC), the football section of which has an international reputation.

Ferencvárosi Torna Club (FTC Budapest)

*Népstadion (People's Stadium)

G/H4/5

Close to the East Station lies the Budapest "Sports Town" with the Népstadion (People's Stadium) as its centre. This arena, built in 1953 to the plans of K. Dávid, covers an area of 17,500 sq. m (20,900 sq. yd). Its stands can accommodate more than 70,000 spectators. It is planned to increase the capacity to 100,000 seats.
Along the Ifjúság útja (Street of Youth), which leads to the stadium, there are notable sculptures on both sides of the road in praise of sport.
Round the stadium are other sporting facilities: the Kisstadion (small stadium; 1962; accommodation 15,000), which has already served as a stage for many show-business artistes; the Millenáris Cycle Race-track (1896), the Nemzeti Sportcsarnok (National Sports Hall (1940)), the Játékcsarnok (Games Hall),

Location
Népstadion út/Ifjúság útja/Verseny útja

Underground Station
M2 (Nepstadion)

Trolleybuses
77, 80

Bus
95

the Testnevelési és Sportmúzeum (Museum of Physical Culture and Sport), the Olimpiaicsarnok (Olympia Hall), the Körcsarnok (Circular Hall) and the ultra-modern Uj Sportcsarnok (New Sports Hall (1981), 12,500 seats), which shortly after its completion became in 1983 the venue of the World Gymnastics Championships.

Nép-sziget

See Angyalföld

New City Hall

See Váci utca

November 7 tér

See Népköztársaság útja

*Óbuda   A–D1/2

Location
District III

HEV line
Batthyány tér–Szentendre

Trams
17, 33

Buses
6, 11, 18, 37, 42, 55, 60, 84, 86, 134, 137, 142, 165, 184

Until its union with Buda and Pest in 1872, Óbuda was a somewhat sleepy little town, but in spite of considerable rebuilding and modernisation it has still managed to retain something of its former atmosphere. This old settlement, where evidence of prehistoric culture has been discovered and where shortly after the birth of Christ the Romans founded their camp of Aquincum, was according to tradition the residence of the Hunnish king Attila in the 5th c. Under the Arpads the place experienced enormous prosperity. In the Middle Ages there was a palace of the Hungarian queens here; in the days of the Turkish occupation the little town on the Danube fell into complete decay, due to the increasing importance of the royal city of Buda. Not until the 17th c. was life restored to the town by German-speaking settlers.

Kiscelli Museum   B1

Location
Kiscelli utca 108

Bus
165

Kiscelli, a part of Óbuda, owes its name to a copy of the miracle-working statue of the Virgin Mary of Mariazell. Here there is a branch of the Historical Museum, housed in rooms of the former Trinitarian monastery (18th c.; architect J. Entzenhoffer). The monastery, which acquired the beautiful Baroque gateway in 1910 designed (1799) by F. A. Hillebrandt for the house of the Jesuit Order in Vienna, has quite recently been thoroughly renovated.

Exhibition

Documents and objects on show provide a good general impression of the economic and cultural life of the three Danube towns of Buda, Óbuda and Pest from the end of the Turkish occupation. Of particular interest are the pictures and accounts of the recovery of Buda by the Austrians in 1686.

Former Synagogue

The former synagogue, which since the Second World War has been used as a cultural centre, was built in the Classical style by A. Landherr between 1820 and 1825. Six pillars and a tympanum with the tablets of the law enhance the main façade.

Location
Lajos utca 16

Óbuda Parish Church (Óbudai plébánia-templom)

C1

This Baroque church was built in the 1740s to plans by J. G. Paur. Inside and in front of the church can be seen fine figures by K. Bebo.

Location
Lajos utca 17

*Zichy Castle (Zichy-kástély)

D1

Commissioned in the middle of the 18th c. by Count Nicholas Zichy, this Baroque castle (architect J. H. Jäger), was severely damaged during the Second World War and has had a lengthy restoration; for some time it has been used as a cultural centre. It houses a local museum and mementoes of Lajos Kassák (1887–1967), the versatile representative of the Hungarian avant-garde. Works by Viktor Vasarely are also on exhibition. From time to time excellent concerts are put on here.
Near by, also in Fő tér, are the Town Hall of Óbuda, the ethnic collection of Zsigmond Kun and a number of very pleasant inns.

Location
Fő tér 1

Opening times
Tue.–Fri. 2 p.m.–6 p.m. Sat., Sun. 10 a.m.–6 p.m.

Flórian tér (Florian Square)

C1

Flórian tér is an important traffic junction. On its north side can be seen ruins of the baths of the Roman legion (Római katonai fürdő maradványai). The bath itself, the sweat-room and the cold-water pool are well preserved. Adjacent is a small museum (documents about the baths and medicine in Roman times; open Tue.–Sun. 10 a.m.–6 p.m.).
At the south edge of the square, in the area of Kálvin Köz, are the remains of the medieval queens' palace and the Reformed church of Óbuda, which was built in the 18th c.

Filatorigát (former silk-mill)

The oval building of the former silk-mill (1785) is now important as an historic industrial building. It commemorates the development of textile production in Óbuda which was demanded by the Emperor Joseph II.

Location
Harrer Pál utca 44–46

Cella trichora (Early Christian graveyard)

The remains of an Early Christian graveyard, laid out in the second half of the 4th c. on a clover-leaf plan, is known as "cella trichora". In the vicinity are ruins dating from the 1st to the 3rd c. A.D.

Location
Corner of Raktár utca/ Hunor utca

Villa of Hercules

In the 1950s and 1960s, the ruins of a magnificent Roman villa (probably dating from the beginning of the 3rd c. A.D.) were

Location
Meggyfa utca 19–21

Óbuda

Aquincum

Entrance

Basilica

Szentendrei út

Árkádena

Great Bath

Archaeological Museum

Market

Floor Mosaic

Mithras Room

Dwelling

Double Bath

Dwelling

Lapidarium

Roman paved streets

20 m
22 yd

Excavation site of the Roman town of Aquincum (1st–4th c. AD) in Obuda in the northern part of Budapest

excavated. The mosaics discovered here, which are among the finest which have ever been found in Hungary, depict scenes from the Hercules myth and the Dionysus legend. The sarcophagi exhibited in the garden of the archaeological museum were made in the 3rd and 4th c. A.D.

*Roman Military Town (Táborvárosi Múzeum)

In 1950 the remains of the military camp, belonging to the Roman town of Aquincum were discovered to the south of Flórián tér. As well as remains of buildings dating from the 2nd to the 4th c., tools, various vessels and sarcophagi were also found. Also of interest are the remains of a hypocaust.

Location
Korvin Ottó utca 63

**Aquincum (plan of excavation see page 103)

The remains of the Roman town of Aquincum, founded in the 1st c. A.D. on the west bank of the Danube, have been systematically excavated since the 1870s. A considerable part of the former municipality is now accessible as a museum.
Opening times: May–Oct. Tues.–Sun. 10 a.m.–6 p.m.

Location
Szentendrei út 139

HEV stop: Aquincum v.m.

About the year 10 B.C. the Romans occupied the territory of their later province of Pannonia. A few years after the birth of Christ they built within the boundaries of Óbuda, now a part of Budapest, a military camp, round which a civil town soon arose, which was to reach its heyday in the 2nd and 3rd c. The flourishing settlement of Aquincum became, as early as the beginning of the 2nd c., the principal town of the province of Pannonia Inferior. The Emperor Septimus Severuss raised it to the status of a "colonia" in A.D. 194.
After the defeat of the Pannonian legions at Hadrianopolis in the year 378 Aquincum declined and the decline was accelerated by increasing and violent attacks by the Barbarians.

History

In the rooms of the Archaeological Museum, opened in 1894, are exhibited cult objects, sculptures, fragments of mosaics, implements, vessels, coins and jewellery. Among the most valuable exhibits are a water-organ of A.D. 288, which has become celebrated, a Jupiter column, a marble Diana and a marble Minerva, a statue of Mithras and a written document dated A.D. 19 (the oldest piece of writing which has until now been found in Hungary); in addition gems and ivory-carving have recently been found.

Archaeological Museum

In the Pillared Hall and in the Lapidarium fine stone-carvings (altars, gravestones, reliefs) can be seen.

Pillared Hall and Lapidarium

The ruins round the museum give an impression of the Roman civil town, some 400 m (440 yd) × 600 m (660 yd) in area, which was laid out according to a plan; as well as numerous and generally one-storeyed private houses it had several large bathing establishments, a market-hall, a Mithras sanctuary and a basilica (probably formerly the "forum").
The provision of water and the sewage system (water-pipes, disposal pipes and heating installations) will be of interest – and not only to specialists.

Ruins in the open

*Amphitheatre of the Roman Military Town

In the 2nd c. A.D. the Romans built a large amphitheatre for their military camp at Aquincum. Its ruins were excavated in 1940. The arena, constructed on an elliptical plan, was 131 m (143 yd) long and 107 m (117 yd) broad, and had room for 15,000 spectators who could enjoy war games here, especially those of a circus-like nature.

Location
Korvin Ottó utca, Corner of
Nagyszombat utca

Archaeological Museum of Aquincum

Some historians have expressed the opinion that the Magyars used this theatre as a fortress in the 9th and 10th c. when they occupied the country.

Amphitheatre of the Roman Civil Town

Location
Diagonally opposite the
Aquincum excavation site

In 1880 and 1937 the remains of the amphitheatre of the civil town of Aquincum were excavated. It originally occupied an area of about 80 m (87 yd) × 90 m (98 yd) and accommodated some 7,500 spectators.

On the opposite side of the road can be seen a restored section of the ancient fortifications of the town.

Opera

See State Opera

Országház

See Parliament Building

Országház utca

See Buda, Important Streets and Squares

*Outer Ring (Nagykörút)

D3–F6(M/N3/4)

The 4 km (2½ mile) long Outer Ring leads from the east end of Margaret Bridge in a half-circle round the city of Pest to the east end of the Petőfi Bridge. It consists of the following sectors: Szent István körút, Marx tér, Lenin körút, November 7 tér, Lenin körút, Blaha Lujza tér, József körút, Ferenc körút, Boráros tér. The ring, which was opened to traffic in 1896 and along which are many imposing buildings dating from the end of the last century, occupies the course of an arm of the Danube which had been filled in, but which in 1867 it was proposed to make navigable for ships.

Trams
4, 6

Buses
12, 12A

Szent István körút (St Stephen's Ring)

D3/4

Szent István körút is the most northerly sector of the Outer Ring. At its west end lie Marx-Engels tér (monument by G. Segesdi, 1971) and Jászai Mari tér, where the Central Committee of the Hungarian Socialist Workers' Party has its headquarters. Further east is the Theatre of Comedy (Vigszínház; No. 14), which in the 1890s was designed by the Viennese architects Fellner and Helmer. The theatre was destroyed in the Second World War but has now been completely rebuilt.

Marx tér (Marx Square)

D4

Marx tér, which from 1978 was redesigned at considerable expense, is also the forecourt of the West Station (Nyugati pályaudvar), a protected building which was erected in the 1870s by the Parisian firm of Eiffel. The first trains on Hungarian territory were run in 1846 from the site now occupied by the West Station.

Underground Station
M3 (Marx tér)

West Station

Lenin körút (Lenin Ring)

D4–F5(M3–N4)

There are a number of notable buildings along Lenin körút. No. 67 is a copy of the Florentine Palazzo Strozzi, designed by A. Hauszmann in 1884 for Count Batthyány; it is now occupied by a register office.

Palais Batthyány

The Hotel Royal (No. 45) was built in the 1890s to plans by the architect Ray. Twenty years ago it was modernised and extended.

Hotel Royal

The Madách Theatre (Madách Szinház; Nos. 29–33) was adapted in 1961 from an existing 19th c. place of entertainment. In this popular theatre can be seen wall-mosaics by the female artist Eszter Mattioni.

Madách Theatre

The Café Hungária (Nos. 9–11) was internationally famous as the Café New York until the Second World War. During the first thirty years of this century, writers, publishers and various well-known personalities used to meet together on the ground floor of the Palais New York built by A. Hauszmann, K. Giergl and F. Korb between 1891 and 1893. The four-storey building in Neo-Renaissance style was severely damaged during the Second World War but has been restored. The refurbished Café Hungária is much admired, especially by tourists from the West. It is a model of Late Eclectic interior architecture.

*Café Hungária

Café Hungária, entrance   *and interior*

Blaha Lujza tér   F5

Underground Station
M2 (Blaha Lujza tér)

This square, situated where the Outer Ring crosses Rákóczi út (see entry), is named after the famous Hungarian actress Lujza Blaha (1850–1926) who had great success in the National Theatre which was formerly situated here.

Palatinus Bathing Beach

See Margaret Island

Parade Ground

See Buda, Important Streets and Squares, Disz tér

Paris Court

See Felszabadulás tér

Parliament Building (Országház)   C/D4(L3)

Location
V, Kossuth Lajos tér

The Parliament Building, which is considered one of the outstanding achievements of modern architecture in the Hungarian capital, was constructed between 1884 and 1904 to plans by Emmerich Steindl. It is situated between Kossuth Lajos tér and the Danube (see entries) and is one of the landmarks of Budapest. The building, which comprises 691 rooms, 8 courtyards and 27 staircases, is 268 m (820 ft) long, up to 118 m (387 ft) wide, and consists of a central range with a dome (96 m (315 ft) high), two 73 m (240 ft) high towers on the loggia facing the Danube, and in addition two side wings; the southern one is the Chamber of the House of Representatives and the northern one the Congress Hall (formerly the Chamber of the Upper House). Each of these chambers is crowned by a roof bearing four turrets. The imposing façade on the bank of the Danube is embellished with eighty-eight statues including Hungarian hereditary princes, military leaders and kings.

On the east side a flight of steps leads up to the main doorway which is flanked by two stone lions. On the ceiling of the stairwell are frescoes by K. Lotz and in a niche a bust of the architect Steindl by A. Stróbl.

On the first floor is the fine domed Hall (height 27 m (88 ft)); the dome is supported on sixteen pillars with likenesses of leading Hungarian rulers. In the Hunting Room (Vadászterem) can be seen wall-paintings by A. Körösföi-Kriesch. Behind this, in the Gobelin Room (Gobelinterem), is a colossal wall tapestry which depicts an assembly of Magyar princes at the time of their occupation of the country. The Chamber of the House of Representatives and the Congress Hall are beautifully decorated. In the Munkácsy Room, next to the study of the leader of the Presidential Council, can be seen the great painting by M. Munkácsy "Conquest of the Country" (by the Magyars).

Underground Station
M2 (Kossuth tér)

Tram
2

Trolleybuses
70, 78

Guided tours
By arrangement (contact Budapest Tourist or IBUSZ)

Interior

The Parliament Building dominates the Danube bank of Pest

The Parliamentary Library (Országgyűlési Könyvtár) has a comprehensive stock of legal, governmental and historical literature; it is reached by the south door on the side of the building facing the Danube.

Parliament Street (Országház utca)

See Buda, Important Streets and Squares

Pauline Monastery

See University Church

People's Park

See Népliget

People's Stadium

See Népstadion

*Pest   C4–F6(K3–N6)

Location
District V

Underground Lines
M1, M2, M3

Trams
2, 2A, 47, 49

Trolleybuses
70, 72, 73, 78, 83

Buses
1, 2, 4, 4A, 5, 7, 7A, 9, 15, 16, 112, 182

Until its union with Buda and Óbuda in 1872, Pest was an independent town, but for a long time its development was difficult, as it was overshadowed by the neighbouring royal town. Nevertheless, for a long time Pest has had close links with Buda. The Romans maintained a "castrum contra Aquincum" at Marcius 15 tér, the purpose of which was to protect the Danube crossing. The Hungarian rulers who resided in Buda visited Pest from time to time to attend services in what is now the Inner City Parish Church (see entry). By the 15th c. Pest had become prosperous. At this period the town was surrounded by fortifications which followed the course of the present Inner Ring.

It was in the 19th c. that Pest attained its greatest prosperity as the town of craftsmen, traders and merchants; this is revealed by the numerous fine buildings which are still standing today. At that time the principal focus of population shifted from the Buda to the Pest side of the Danube. As early as 1830 there were far more than 60,000 people in Buda, the majority of them living in the rapidly growing suburbs. The inner city of Pest forms the central business district of the Hungarian capital. Pest is the headquarters of the most important organs of government, Parliament (see entry), ministries, etc., and leading cultural institutions (universities, museums, churches, etc.).

Pest Broadway

See Nagymező utca

Pest Danube Bank

See Danube Corso

Pest District Council

See Municipal Council

Pest Redoubt

See Vigadó

Pest Synagogue   E5(M4)

The Pest Synagogue was built between 1854 and 1859 to the plans of the Viennese architect Ludwig Förster. The romanticised Moorish-Byzantine style of this three-aisled temple is very pleasing; F. Feszl was responsible for the fine interior.

The Jewish Museum (Országos Zsidó Vallási és Történeti Gyűjtemény) is housed in an annexe of the synagogue; it contains interesting documentation and valuable works of art. On Wesselényi utca is a heroes' temple (1931) for the Jewish soldiers who fell in the First World War.
In the synagogue garden can be seen a cemetery with a memorial to the victims of National Socialism.

Location
VII, Dohány utca 2

Underground Station
M2 (Astoria)

Trolleybus
74

Opening times
Tues., Wed., Fri., Sun.
10 a.m.–1 p.m.; Mon., Thur.
2–6 p.m.

Pest Theatre

See Váci utca

*Petőfi Museum (Petőfi Irodalmi Múzeum)   E5/6(M5)

The museum is dedicated to Sándor Petőfi (1823–1849) and contains memorabilia and a collection of texts of the leading Hungarian poet and author. There are journals, manuscripts, books, periodicals, etc., a sound archive and works by various notable artists. From time to time exhibitions on particular themes and on the subject of selected Hungarian authors (including Miklós Radnóti) add to the interest.

The Petőfi Museum is housed in the historical Károlyi Palace, a 19th c. building in Classical style. In 1848/49 the Austrian General Julius Haynau, who was to defeat the freedom fighters, resided here. It was here, too, that Count Lajos Batthyány was arrested in 1848. Mihály Károlyi (1875–1955), politician and Hungarian President from 1918 to 1919, was the owner of this palace. A memorial room has been furnished in his honour.

Location
VI, Károlyi Mihály utca 16

Bus
15

Opening times
Tues.–Sun. 10 a.m.–6 p.m.

Károlyi Palace

Petőfi Sándor utca   D5(M4/5)

Petőfi Sándor utca, formerly called Uri utca (Gentlemen's Walk), one of the fine highways of Pest, joins the two squares

Buses
2, 15

Felszabadulás tér and Martinelli tér (see entries). Together with Váci utca (see entry) and the adjoining streets it forms the principal shopping centre of the Hungarian capital. Buildings notable for their architecture are house No. 3 which dates from the 19th c. to the plans of J. Hild and No. 6, the popular József Katona Theatre (Katona József Színház). Close by (Nos. 13–19) is the Budapest Main Post Office and Telegraph Office.

Petőfi tér   D5(L5)

Location
District V

Tram: 2

Buses: 2, 15

This square, named after the Hungarian lyric poet Sándor Petőfi (see Notable Personalities) is the venue of the patriotic festivities which take place annually on 15 March. There is a well-proportioned bronze Petőfi monument by Adolf Huszár (1882) in the square.

Greek church

On the east side of Petőfi tér is the three-aisled Greek church (Orthodox Egyház templom), erected in 1789 and rebuilt in the 19th c. to the plans of Ybl. Inside this large church there are fine works of art by Nikolaus Jankovits, Anton Kochmeister and others.

Pharmaceutical Museum "Golden Eagle"

See Buda, Important Streets and Squares, Tárnok utca

Plague Column

See Buda, Important Streets and Squares, Szentháromság tér

Planetarium

See Népliget

Postal Museum

See Népköztársaság útja

Postal Savings Bank

See Szabadság tér

Premonstratensian Convent

See Margaret Island

Prince Eugene Equestrian Statue

See Castle Palace

Puppet Theatre

See Népköztársaság útja

Rác-fürdo (Rac Baths)

See Tabán

Rákóczi út

E/F5(M/N4)

This thoroughfare, named after Prince Rákóczi, the leader of the independence movement of the beginning of the 18th c. (see Notable Personalities), is a continuation of Kossuth Lajos utca, from the site of the now-vanished medieval Hatvan town gate on the Inner Ring (see entry) to the East Station (see entry). Rákóczi út, today one of the main shopping streets of Budapest, is flanked by many large stores (Textiljáz, Verseny, Csillag, Lottó and Otthon), and important cultural institutions, for example the Academy of Stage and Film Art (Szinmüvészeti Föiskola) and the associated Odry Theatre (Odry színpad) at Vas utca. In addition there are leading cinemas (Uránia, No. 21; Tisza, No. 70) and well-known restaurants and cafés (Restaurant Emke, Konditorei Hauer, etc.).
Secular buildings notable for their architecture are No. 5 (1867; formerly a hotel; memorial tablet to Prince Rákóczi) and No. 13 which was built in 1837 to plans by J. Hild.

Location
Boundary between Districts VII and VIII

Underground Stations
M2 (Astoria, Keleti pu)

Buses
7, 7A, 78

The Baroque St Rochus Chapel (Rókus-kápolna) was built in 1711 and extended in 1740. Its tower dates from the end of the 18th c.
Near the chapel is the Rochus Hospital (Rókus-kórház) where Ignaz Philipp Semmelweis (see Notable Personalities) worked between 1851 and 1857. His statue was created in Carrara marble by A. Stróbl.

St Rochus Chapel

Redoubt

See Vigadó

Reformed Churches

See Inner Ring, Kálvin tér, China Museum

Roman Excavations

See Óbuda, Március 15 tér

*Roosevelt tér

D5(L4)

The double square at the Pest end of the Chain Bridge commemorates the former US President Franklin D. Roosevelt. At

Location
District V

111

Tram
2

Buses
2, 15, 16

the beginning of the last century markets were held here. Also, until the Chain Bridge was built, there was a mooring-place for Danube freighters. On the northern side of the square stands a memorial to Széchenyi by J. Engel (1880) and on the south side a Deák memorial by the artist A. Huszár (1882).

*Gresham Palace (Gresham-palota)   D5(L4)

Location
V, east side of Roosevelt tér

One of the masterpieces of Secessionist style in Budapest is the Gresham Palace built in 1907 to plans by Quittner and the Vágó brothers. This traditional former insurance building is now the seat of the Municipal Tourist Office of Budapest (Budapest Tourist).
Between the two world wars the former Café Gresham was a well-known meeting-place for artists.

*Hungarian Academy of Science   D5(L4)
(Magyar Tudományos Akadémia)

Location
V, north side of Roosevelt tér

The north side of Roosevelt tér is dominated by the monumental building of the Hungarian Academy of Science; in Neo-Renaissance style, it was founded on the initiative of Count Istvan Széchenyi (see Notable Personalities) in 1825. The headquarters of this, now the most eminent scientific institution in Hungary, was completed in 1864. Plans were drawn by the Berlin architect Friedrich August Stüler. The façades of the building are embellished with artistic representations. Also of interest is a bronze relief by Holló (1893) which depicts the foundation of the Academy by Count Széchenyi in 1825.

Hungarian Academy of Science in Roosevelt Square

The Academy, with which there are now associated a number of research institutes, has a scientific library which is well known even outside the frontiers of the country (especially the Oriental Department). In the restored Festival Hall are fine frescoes by K. Lotz.

North-east of the Academy stand two notable Classical buildings: at Akadémia utca 1, completed in 1835 (fine façade with Corinthian wall pillars), there once lived the Polish General József Bem and György Klapka, both renowned fighters in the freedom struggle of 1848/49. Near by at Akadémia utca 3 is an imposing building dating from 1836 by the great architect J. Hild.

Akadémia utca

Eötvös tér

D5(L4)

Adjoining Roosevelt tér on the south is the small Eötvös tér with a monument of József Eötvös (see Notable Personalities) by A. Huszár. On the south side of the square stand two luxury hotels, Atrium Hyatt and Forum, which were opened comparatively recently.

Location
V, south of Roosevelt tér

*Rose Hill (Rózsadomb)

B/C3

Rose Hill (Rózsadomb; District II) has long been one of the most exclusive residential areas of the Hungarian capital. Elegant villas, large gardens, avenues and footpaths extend to the Cool Valley (Hüvövöly). On the side of the hill facing the Danube a modern trade union convalescent home is visible from a considerable distance.

Location
II, west of Margaret Bridge

Buses
11, 91, 191

Turbe of Gül Baba (Gül Baba türbeje)

C3

In the grounds of an old villa can be found the Turbe (mausoleum) of a Muslim Dervish Gül Baba (Turkish = rose father), which was built between 1543 and 1548. Gül Baba died during a festival in the Matthias Church which had been converted into a mosque. The rather plain octagonal domed building is now a museum (open Tues.–Sun. 10 a.m.–6 p.m.; memorials of Gül Baba and the Bektasi Order).

Location
Mecset utca 14

Trams
4, 6, 17

Buses
91, 191

Rottenbill Park

See Köbánya

Rudas Bath

See Gellért Hill

St Andrew (St Andreas)

See Szentendre

St Anne's Church

See Viziváros

St Elisabeth's Church

See Viziváros

St Joseph's Church

See Joseph Town Parish Church

St Nicholas' Tower

See Buda, Important Streets and Squares, Hess András tér

St Rochus Chapel

See Rákóczi ut

*St Stephen's Basilica (Szent István-bazilika)   D5(M4)

Location
V, Szent István tér

Underground Station
M1 (Bajcsy Zsilinszky út)

Buses
4, 4A, 6, 16

St Stephen's Basilica, in Neo-Renaissance style, is one of the most imposing ecclesiastical buildings of the Hungarian capital. The church is of monumental proportions with a central dome, 96 m (315 ft) high, and two 80 m (262 ft) high towers at the west end. Building began in 1851. The plans were largely the work of József Hild, the great exponent of Classical architecture. After Hild's death and the collapse of the dome in 1868, Miklós Ybl proposed new plans which finally gave the church its great size and Neo-Renaissance style. After Ybl's death in 1905 Jozsef Kauser completed St Stephen's Church, which was recently restored at considerable cost.

Interior

Magnificent works of art adorn the interior: by the first pillar on the right supporting the dome can be seen a group of figures by A. Stróbl which portray Bishop Gellért and St Emmerich. On the second pillar on the right is King Ladislaus the Holy, a work of János Fadrusz; on the second pillar on the left there is a statue of St Elisabeth by K. Senyci. The mosaics on the dome were produced in the Salviati workshop in Venice to sketches by Karl Lotz. At the magnificent High Altar is a statue of St Stephen made of Carrara marble by A. Stróbl. On the wall of the apse the bronze reliefs by E. Mayer depict scenes from the life of St Stephen, and the pictures in the side altars are also very fine. Of particular note is the painting on the second altar to the right of the main entrance. It is a work by Gyula Benczúr and shows St Stephen offering the Hungarian crown to Mary.

Fessler Statues

The Fessler statues are one of the special features of St Stephen's Basilica. On the exterior wall of the apse the Twelve

St Stephen's Basilica

State Opera House, interior

Apostles can be seen; the Four Evangelists stand in niches on the outside of the dome; in niches on the towers of the main façade are likenesses of the Fathers of the Church and in the tympanum of the narthex the Patrona Hungariae, surrounded by Hungarian saints.

Semmelweis Museum

See Tabán

Semmelweis University

See Üllői út

Serbian Church

See Váci utca

Sigmund Square

See Zsigmond tér

Silk Spinning Mill

See Óbuda

South Station (Déli pályaudvar)   B5(L7)

Location
1, Alkotás utca-Krisztina körút

Underground Station
M2 (Déli pu.).

The very modern South Station was completed in 1977 to plans by the architect G. Kővári. It is the terminus for trains from Lake Balaton (see entry) and from southern Transdanubia. In the semi-circular station forecourt – terminus of underground (Metro) line 2 – is a work in enamel by Viktor Vasarély.
Trams 18, 59, 61. Buses 5, 12, 21, 39.

Meadow of Blood

On the north side of the station lies an open space which in 1795 became known as the "Meadow of Blood" (Vermező), where the instigators of the Hungarian Jacobin movement were executed. On the north side of the present park a monument commemorates this event. After the Second World War the area was raised about 2 m (6 ft) with debris and laid out as a park, in the centre of which is an anti-Fascist memorial by I. Szabó (1967).

Christinatown Parish Church

In Krisztina tér, south-east of the South Station stands the Christinatown Parish Church (Krisztina-városi plébánia-templom) which was built in the 18th c.

Spa Establishments

See Practical Information

Square of 15 March

See Március 15 tér

Stadium

See Népstadion

*State Opera (Allami Operaház)   D/E4(M3)

Location
VI, Népköztársaság útja 22

Underground Station
M1 (Opera)

Buses
1, 4, 4A

Miklós Ybl drew up the plans for the prestigious State Opera, which was built between 1875 and 1884 in Neo-Renaissance style.
Arcades, which bear a balcony with balustrades, protect the carriage entrance. In the two niches on either side are statues of Franz Liszt and Ferenc Erkels, the first Director of the opera, by A. Stróbl.
On the first storey of the main façade is a loggia; in each of the two corner pillars two allegorical figures have been let in. On the balustrade of the first storey are statues of famous composers by the Hungarian artists G. Donáth, G. Kiss and A. Stróbl.

Interior

The interior of the State Opera boasts a magnificent foyer with a double marble staircase. B. Székely created the ceiling-frescoes; the wall-paintings portraying scenes from Greek mythology are the work of Mór Than. A. Stróbl fashioned the bust of Ybl.

The auditorium boasts unusually good acoustics. The Royal Box, which has been restored to its original form, and the retiring-room are redolent of the elegance of yester-year. The ceiling-frescoes by K. Lotz and the wall-paintings by Mór Than are masterpieces of their kind.

Opposite the Opera is the State Ballet Institute (Allami Ballett-intézet), which was created in 1883 to plans by the architects Lechner and Pártos.

State Ballet Institute

Street of the People's Republic

See Népköztársaság útja

Szabadság hid

See Freedom Bridge

*Szabadság tér (Freedom Square)

D4(L3)

Freedom Square, laid out in the last century after a barracks where many Hungarian freedom fighters of 1848/49 were executed was pulled down, forms with the surrounding buildings one of the most charming architectural ensembles of Budapest. On its west side stands the former Exchange, now the headquarters of Hungarian Television; on the east side is the Hungarian National Bank (Magyar Nemzeti Bank). Both these functional buildings were the work of the architect Ignác Alpár and date from 1905. The former Exchange is in Secessionist style, while the National Bank is a first-class example of a Late Classical building.

In the centre of the semicircular northern end of the square stands a Soviet memorial (obelisk) with a relief by the artist Károly Antal (1945). The northern arc is lined by buildings in the Neo-Romanesque-Eclectic manner.

Location
District V

Underground Station
M2 (Kossuth tér)

Bus
15

National Bank

Near the bank, but oriented towards Rosenberg házaspár utca, is the former Postal Savings Bank (No. 4) by Ödön Lechner, who was here anxious to create a new Hungarian architectural style. The building, which was opened in 1901, is characterised by variegated majolica decoration from the porcelain factory at Pécs.

Former Postal Savings Bank

Széchenyi-lanchid

See Chain Bridge

Széchenyi National Library

See Castle Palace

Székesfehérvár (Stuhlweissenburg)

Székesfehérvár, known as Stuhlweissenburg when the royal family was on the throne, is the oldest town in Hungary. It

Location: 65 km (40 miles) south-west of Budapest

Székesfehérvár (Stuhlweissenburg)

received its charter from King Stephen I, and for almost 300 years it remained the royal seat, under the name of Alba Regia. It came under Turkish rule in 1543, when a large part of the medieval buildings were destroyed. From the 17th c. onwards it enjoyed a revival. Having suffered heavy damage during the Second World War, Székesfehérvár has developed into a modern industrial town, home of the Videoton Hi-Fi works, the Ikarus Coachworks and aluminium factories, etc.

Places to visit

The Gothic Chapel of St Anne is the sole surviving medieval building. There are only a few ruins left of the old royal seat. A fine collection of Baroque buildings house the bishop's palace, the town-hall, the Zichy palace and the Franciscan convent. On Szabadság tér can found remains of the 11th c. royal basilica; other buildings worth a visit are the cathedral with its two towers, completed in 1771, the Black Eagle chemist's shop (museum) with its splendid Rococo interior and the King Stephen Museum on Gargarin tér.

Széna tér (Hay Square)

See Moszkva tér

*Szentendre (St Andrew)

Location
20 km (12 miles) north of Budapest

Access
HEV line
Budapest-Szentendre.
In summer boats from
Budapest (Vigadó tér)

The romantic little town of Szentendre (101 m (331 ft); pop. 16,000) is situated on the hilly right bank of the Danube to the north of Budapest. In the past many artists were attracted within its boundaries. Meanwhile tourists have also "discovered" the town.

The origins of the settlement go back to the 4th c. B.C. when the Celts were here. About the time of Christ's birth the Romans set up a military camp. The first mention of the place is in 1146 and

Szentendre
Town Centre

1 Merchant's Cross

2 Picture Gallery

3 Blagoveštenska Church

4 Margit-Kovács Collection

5 Ferenczy Museum

6 Museum of Serbian Ecclesiastical Art

7 Cultural Centre

100 m
110 yd

from the 14th c. several waves of Serbs arrived. In the 18th c. Szentendre experienced an economic upsurge (trade centre) and became a Pravo-Slav bishopric.

The chief square in Szentendre is the triangular Marx tér, in which stands an 18th c. merchants' cross, a masterpiece of wrought-iron work. The square is preserved as an historical monument.

Sights
Marx tér

On the Danube side of this square is the Greek Orthodox Blagoveštenska Church which was built in the middle of the 18th c. to plans by Andreas Mayerhoffer. It contains an iconostasis in Rococo style. On the north adjoining the church is the Ferenczy Károly Múzeum (Marx tér 6), with works by the artist family of Ferenczy (paintings, sculptures, tapestries) and numerous exhibits of local history (archaeological finds, Hungarian and Serbian costumes, etc.).

Blagoveštenska Church

On the south side of the Blagoveštenska Church can be found the collection of the ceramic artist Margit Kovács (d. 1977) who combined traditional popular art and modern elements in her work.

Margit-Kovács Collection

Above Marx tér on Várdomb Castle Hill (fine views) stands the Roman Catholic church, the origins of which go back to a 13th c. building. Parts of the present, predominately 18th c., church are of 14th and 15th c. dates. The interior contains modern frescoes. Opposite the church the works of the painter Béla Czóbel (1883–1976) are presented in a fitting setting.

Roman Catholic Parish Church

The Serbian Orthodox Episcopal church, which was completed in 1764 is situated in the upper part of Alkótmány utca. Its

Serbian Orthodox Episcopal Church

Szentendre, inner town

Detail in the Skanzen open-air Museum

Szentháromság tér

Rococo doorway and the fine carving of the iconastasis are worthy of note. In the courtyard a collection of Serbian Church art (Szerb Egyházmǔvészeti Gyǔjtemény) can be seen.

Cultural Centre

Nearby on the north in Engels utca is the Cultural Centre (Mǔvelǒdési Központ és Könyvtár), with a fine mosaic by Jenǒ Barcsay. Close to the Centre is an art gallery showing works by Margit Anna and Imre Ámos.

Town Hall

To the south of Castle Hill is the Baroque Town Hall (Városi Tanács) and the 18th c. Catholic Church of Peter and Paul (Péter-Pál-templom) which is the successor to a Pravo-Slav Ciprovačka Church.

Požarevačka Church

Along the road from the town centre southwards to the HEV Station is the Baroque Požarevačka Church, dedicated in 1763; this is a Greek Orthodox church with a wonderful icon wall in Byzantine style. To the south-west of this church in Római Sánc utca are the remains of a former Roman camp.

Preobraženska Church

To the north of Marx tér in Vörös Hadsereg útja stands the Serbian Orthodox Preobraženska Church, built in 1740, which is one of the finest Pravo-Slav churches in Szentendre. Further

Artists' Colony

to the north is an artists' colony which came into being in 1928 and where today more than three dozen artists are busy. Periodic exhibitions can be seen in an adjoining gallery.

*Open-air Museum
Skanzen

About 3 km (2 miles) north of the town centre is the folklore museum of Skanzen which is still being developed, where rural buildings, houses, mills, churches and other architectural features from various regions of Hungary have been re-erected in their original style. Inside some of the buildings can be seen traditional furnishings and articles of everyday use and this enables the visitor to gain a comprehensive idea of life in provincial Hungary.

Leányfalu

A few kilometres north of Szentendre lies the first-class holiday resort of Leányfalu (a boating harbour on the Danube, camping site, bathing beaches, etc.) which was popular with artists and men of letters as early as the beginning of the 19th c.

Szentháromság tér

See Buda, Important Streets and Squares

Szentháromság utca

See Buda, Important Streets and Squares

Szent István körút

See Outer Ring

*Tabán   C5/6(M/N8)

Location
District I

The district of Tabán lies in the depression between Castle Hill and Gellért Hil (see entry). During the time of the Turkish occu-

120

pation Tamils particularly were settled here. In the 18th c. there was an influx of Serbian refugees whose simple dwellings were removed between the two world wars.
Extensive parks and traffic layouts are features of the modern district.

*Semmelweis Museum (Semmelweis Orvostörténeti Múzeum)

C5(N8)

At the foot of Castle Hill on the south-east side stands the 18th c. house (renovated in the 19th c.) in which the famous Hungarian doctor, Ignaz Philipp Semmelweis (see Notable Personalities) was born. It is now furnished as a museum of the history of medicine and includes documents and objects left by Ignaz Philipp Semmelweis, medical implements and instruments and pharmaceutical utensils.

Location
1, Apród utca 1–3

*Golden Stag (Arany Szarvas)

C5(N8)

This famous old inn is furnished in the "pigtail" style of the 19th c. From this triangular building steps lead up to the castle which still has some pretty architectural details of the last century.

Location
1, Szarvas tér 1

*Tabán Parish Church (Tabáni plébánia-templom)

C5(N8)

This Baroque church with only a single tower is dedicated to St Catherine of Alexandria. It was built between 1728 and 1740 and replaced a medieval church which existed at that time and which, during the Turkish occupation, was known as the Mustafa Mosque.
One of the treasures of the Tabán Parish Church is a carved figure (called the "Tabán Christ") below the gallery. It is a copy of a figure dating from the 12th c. and the original can be seen in the Castle Museum, below the gallery. In a niche is a representation of St Florian, no doubt inspired by the disastrous conflagration of Tabán in 1810. The frescoes were the work of Kimnach (1890).

Location
1, Szarvas tér

Ybl Miklós tér (Nicholas Ybl Square)

C5(N8)

Below the castle on the bank of the Danube lies the square named after the famous architect Nicholas (Miklós) Ybl (1814–91). His monument in the centre of the square was the work of E. Mayer (1896). Round the square stand buildings designed by Ybl and he was also responsible for the splendid flight of steps (1882), with arcades and niches, which leads up to the castle. The 310 m (340 yd) long castle bazaar (Várbazár) always attracts many tourists to its shops, artists' studios and inns. In the warm months of the year dancing and entertainment take place on its terrace.

Location
1, Danube Bank

Rác-fürdó (Emmerich Baths, Imre-fürdó)

C5(N8)

The Rac Baths which are situated to the south of Tabán Parish Church were established and extended in the Turkish period. The medicinal springs were known as early as the 15th c.

Location
1, Hadnagy utca

Tanács körút

See Inner Ring

Táncsics Mihály utca

See Buda, Important Streets and Squares

Tárnok utca

See Buda, Important Streets and Squares

Terézváros (Theresa's Town)   D–F4/5(M/N3/4)

Location
District V

Underground Station
M2 (Opera, Hósok tere)

This former suburb of Pest has managed to retain its character of the first half of the 19th c.

Along Majakovszkij utca can be seen an exemplary range of Classical dwellings. Of especial merit is the former house of a goldsmith (No. 11), dating from 1810 with an articulated façade. Farther on is a building (No. 47) designed by A. Pollack in 1848, which is in the Romantic style.

Theresa Town Parish Church   E4/5(N3)
(Terézvárosi plébánia-templom)

Location
Corner of Majakovszkij/
Nagymezó utca

Trolleybuses
70, 78

This church was built to designs by F. Kasselik at the beginning of the 19th c. Originally it was in "pigtail" style but a few decades later it was rebuilt in Neo-Baroque. The High Altar by M. Pollack is of special merit. The beautiful chandelier formerly hung in the Pest Redoubt (see Vigadó).

Theatre of Comedy

See Outer Ring, Szent István körút

Thermal Spa Hotel

See Margaret Island

Tolbuhin tér

See Inner Ring

Transport Museum

See City Woodland Park

Trinity Square

See Buda, Important Streets and Squares

Trinity Street

See Buda, Important Streets and Squares

Ujlak Parish Church (Ujlaki plébánia-templom)   C2

The Baroque Parish Church of Ujlak, a settlement which was in existence in the Middle Ages as an independent community, was built in the 18th c. to plans by Chr. Hamom and M. Nepauer. On the High Altar which is the work of Hickisch can be seen a picture by Falconer and a copy of a "Madonna" by Lukas Cranach.

Location
II, corner Bécsi út/Szép-völgyi út

Tram
17

Üllői út   E6–J8(N5/6)

Üllői út leads from Kálvin tér (see entry) along an arterial road to the south-east. The section near the centre is flanked by a number of very well-maintained Classical buildings. Of especial note are No. 7, No. 17 which was the work of M. Pollack and M. Ybl and once the residence of the composer Ferenc Erkel, and some older buildings of the Budapest Clinic. South-east of the Museum of Applied Arts (see entry) with its notable architecture, are buildings of the turn of the century as well as other departments of the clinic.

Location
Boundary between Districts VIII, IX and X

Underground Stations
M3 (Kálvin tér, Népliget)

Bus
182

Kun Béla tér, which is hemmed in between buildings of the clinic and the Botanical Garden of the University (see entry) has a particular charm because of the monument unveiled in 1967 commemorating three of the prominent leaders of the Hungarian-Societ Republic (Béla Kun, Jeno Landler and Tibor Szamuely); the monument was a combined work by the artists A. Farkas, K. Herczeg and Z. O. Kiss.

Kun Béla tér

On Nagyvárad tér farther south-east, a twenty-three-storey building is one of the tallest landmarks of the Hungarian capital. In it a number of important departments of the Semmelweis University of Medicine are housed.
Opposite to the south is the clinic of the district of Ferencváros with the Cardiological Institute. There are a number of sports grounds in the vicinity.

Semmelweis University

Underground Railway Museum

See Inner Ring, Deák Ferenc tér

Union Monument

See Margaret Island

Universities

Karl Marx University	See Dimitrov tér
Loránd-Eötvös University	See entry
Semmelweis University	See Üllői út

*University Church (Egyetemi templom)   D/E6 (M5)

Location
V, Eötvös Loránd utca 5–7

Bus
15

The University Church, probably the most beautiful Baroque church in Budapest, was built between 1725 and 1742 to plans by Andreas Mayerhoffer for the Pauline Order established in Hungary. Its two mighty towers were completed in 1770/71. The principal façade includes a triangular gable with a representation of the hermits Paul and Anthony as well as the arms of the Pauline Order (a palm between two lions and a raven).

Interior

The University Church has a nave and a side chapel. The frescoes on the ceiling (scenes from the life of Mary) are the work of a J. Bergl (1776). The choir-stalls and the sculptures of the nativity of Mary together with St Paul and St Anthony were carved by Jozsef Hebenstreit (1746). The copy of the "Black Madonna from Tschenstochau" was probably completed about 1720.
Pauline monks of various workshops were responsible for the pulpit, the pews, the doors and the sacristy cupboards which are decorated with intarsia work. The cupboards contain valuable monstrances, chalices and ecclesiastical vestments.

Pauline Monastery

The former Pauline Monastery near the church (18th c.; architect: Matthias Drenker) has housed since 1805 the Theological Faculty of the first Hungarian University which was transferred in 1784 to Pest.
The library, finished in 1775, has richly decorated bookcases, a gallery running round it and a spiral staircase with pierced balustrades and banisters. The ceiling-fresco was created by Pietro Rivetti in 1803.

Úri utca

See Buda, Important Streets and Squares.

*Vác

Location
34 km (21 miles) north of Budapest

Access
By rail from Budapest, Nyugati pu.

The town of Vác (111 m (364 ft); pop. 34,000) lies on the strip of land between the northern Hungarian Uplands and the Alfold. It was already a bishopric in the 11th c. It suffered greatly during the Turkish occupation and lost almost all its medieval buildings. In 1846 the first railway in Hungary was opened between Vác and Budapest. Today Vác is a thriving industrial town (building materials, chemicals, shipbuilding).

Sights
Cathedral

The main square of Vác is Konstantin tér, laid out in the Baroque style. Here the Cathedral stands, (1763–77) built to plans of I. Canevale; its beautiful frescoes in the dome and the murals in the choir are the work of the artist Maulbertsch. In the Cathedral Treasury notable goldsmiths' work of the Renaissance and the Baroque periods can be seen. Opposite the cathedral is the Bishop's Palace of 1775 and to the south the Vak-Bottyán Museum (Múzeum utca 4) which contains exhibits concerning the history of the town.

Vak-Bottyán Museum

Not far north of the cathedral lies Trinity Square with a beautiful Trinity Column dedicated in 1755. On the east side of the square is a Baroque church (18th c.), the origins of which go back to a church of the Piarists.

Trinity Square

The Square of 15 March, formerly the town market-place, is surrounded by fine Baroque buildings. The imposing Parish Church of the Upper Town (Felsővárosi plébánia-templom; 18th c.) has Rococo elements. Close by stands the 18th c. Town Hall (Városi Tanácsház; 18th c.) and the Deaf and Dumb Institute, dating from 1802.

Square of 15 March

In the north of the Inner Town in Köztársaság útja rises a Triumphal Gate designed by I. Canevale in 1764 commemorating the Empress Maria Theresa.

Triumphal Gate

Some 11 km (7 miles) south-east of Vác near Vácrátót is the arboretum of the Hungarian Academy of Science, in a park extending over 24 ha (59 acres), laid out in the last century. In the park several thousand species of trees can be studied.

Surroundings

*Váci utca

D5/6(L/M4/5)

Váci utca leads from Vörösmarty tér (see entry) first to Felszabadulás tér (see entry) and on to Dimitrov tér (see entry). Its northern sector is the city's leading shopping street (partly pedestrianised). Here there is a succession of stores, boutiques, footwear and leather shops, bookshops, jewellers, arts and crafts shops, expressos and the offices of the leading airline companies. The International Trade Centre is also to be found on the Váci utca.

Location
District V

Underground Stations
M1, M2, M3 (Deák tér) M3 (Felszabadulás tér)

The Pest Theatre (Pesti Színház; No. 9) occupies the former "Hotel of the Seven Electoral Princes", where the eleven-year-old Franz Liszt gave his first concert in Pest in 1823. The foyer of the theatre with its beautiful dark mosaic work is very impressive.

Pest Theatre

The new Town Hall (Uj Városház; Nos. 62–64) was built by the architect E. Steindl in Neo-Renaissance style between 1869 and 1875. There are wonderful mosaics by K. Lotz in the Council Chamber.

New Town Hall

The Serbian church (Szerb templo), on the corner of Veres Pálné and Szěb u., was probably designed by the famous architect Andreas Mayerhoffer in the 18th c. Especially impressive is its façade with a single high tower. The nave has three articulated parts. The women's section on a higher level is separated from the men's section by a wooden balustrade. Higher still lies the Solea with the seat of the prelate. The iconostasis, which divides the choir from the nave, was painted in the middle of

Serbian Church

Váci utca

Vigadó, interior

the 19th c. by K. Sterio and is characterised by features showing the influence of Italian Renaissance paintings. The church is closed at the present time.

Vajdahunyad

See City Woodland Park

Városliget

See City Woodland Park

Városmajor (Municipal Farm, Park)   A/B4

Location
XII, Szilágyi Erzsébet Fasor-Városmajor utca

Buses
5, 18, 22, 28, 56, 56E, 128

Városmajor Park, about 10 ha (25 acres) in extent has tennis-courts, games areas and footpaths, and on fine days attracts very many citizens of Budapest seeking relaxation. The old trees, which were planted here more than a century ago, are a particularly charming feature.

Hotel Budapest

On the north side of the park is the Hotel Budapest, an imposing circular tower block (18 storeys, 560 beds) designed by G. Szrogh.

Cog-wheel Railway

A cog-wheel railway (Fogaskerekű vasút) in the western part of the park ascends to Széchenyi-hegy from which there are panoramic views.

In the eastern part of Városmajor Park is an open-air theatre with more than 1000 seats for spectators, as well as a Catholic church, designed by A. and B. Arkay, which has frescoes by V. Aba-Novák and stained-glass windows by L. Arkay.

On Városmajor utca, south of the park, can be seen houses built in Romantic and Classical styles.

Várpalota

See Castle Palace

Vidám Park

See City Woodland Park, Pleasure park

Villa of Hercules

See Óbuda

Vienna Gate Square

See Buda, Important Streets, and Squares, Bécsi kapu tér

Vigadó, façade overlooking the Danube

*Vigadó (Pest Redoubt)

Location
V, Vigadó tér

Underground Station
M1 (Vörösmarty tér)

Tram
2

Buses
2, 15

Boat Landing Stage
Vigadó

The Vigadó built 1859 to plans by Frigyes Feszl, is among the most remarkable examples of Hungarian Romantic architecture. Intended for festival occasions and all kinds of musical entertainment, the Vigadó was severely damaged at the end of the Second World War, but after very many years of restoration it was again opened in 1980.

The side of the Pest Redoubt facing the Danube is exceptionally noteworthy: each of the two projecting sections on the flanks is borne on two pillars topped with crowns, with representations of King Béla IV and historical female figures. On the upper floor of the centre range, between the tall arched windows, can be seen allegorical figures. Above the window arches are a frieze with the Hungarian coat of arms, figures of the two kings Louis I and Matthias Corvinus by János Hunyadi and Miklós Zrinyi, as well as statues of the Palatine Jószef and Count Széchenyi. In the Vigadó Gallery are exhibitions of works by famous artists. On the square in front of the Vigadó stands the Soviet monument and on the south side of Vigadó tér the luxury hotel, Duna Intercontinental.

**Visegrád

Location
42 km/30 miles north of Budapest

Visegrád (108 m (354 ft), pop. 2500) has an exceptionally picturesque situation on the loop of the Danube in the Hungarian Wachau and is one of the most-visited tourist venues in Hungary.

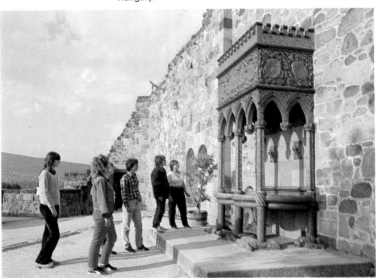

Wall fountain in the Royal Palace of Visegrád

Visegrád
Royal Palace
Királyi palota

1 Foundation of Grand Staircase

2 New Staircase

3 Corridor

4 Hercules Fountain (red marble)

5 Gothic Cloister

6 North Rock Court

7 North Steps

8 Bath

9 Lion Fountain

10 Cellar

11 Great Hall in Beatrix Palace

The Romans maintained a fortification at this strategically favourable place; there is a reconstruction of a watch-tower near Fő utca. In the 9th c. A.D. the Slavs settled here (Slav "Višegrad" = elevated fortress). Later the Magyars pressed forward and occupied the fortress. Right up to the 14th c. the Hungarian Royal Crown was kept in the stronghold.

Above Fő utca in the north of Visegrád are the remains of a King's Palace which was begun in the first half of the 14th c. and which, with its sumptuous buildings and courtyards, once covered an area of 600 m (660 yds) × 300 m (330 yds). The palace was extended by Kings Charles Robert of Anjou, Sigismund of Luxemburg and Matthias I. Corvinus and was finally completed by Italian builders. Altogether it is said to have had 350 rooms and to have been very richly furnished. At the end of the 17th c. the palace was unoccupied and gradually decayed. In 1934 the architect Schulek strove to preserve what was left of the Gothic and Renaissance building of the former royal residence.

Solomon's Tower (originally 30 m (98 ft) high) was erected in the 13th c. and is a mighty relic of the lower castle of Visegrád; the walls are up to 8 m (26 ft) thick! From this hexagonal tower a wall extends to the bastion on the bank of the Danube. The name of the tower probably comes from a previous building in which King Solomon is said to have been kept prisoner in the 11th c.

Access
Bus and boat from Budapest

Sights
King's Palace
(Királyi palota)

Solomon's Tower
(Salamon-torony)

Viziváros

King Matthias Museum

Solomon's Tower is now used as the King Matthias Museum. It contains very well-preserved artefacts from the ruined King's Palace, for example, floor tiles and part of a Hercules Fountain.

Stronghold/Citadel (Fellygvár)

High above the Danube at an elevation of 315 m (1034 ft; footpath and panoramic road) on a site from which there are splendid views, stand the mighty ruins of the Visegrád Stronghold, built on a triangular plan. Building began in 1241 after the attack by the Tartars, that is in the time of King Béla IV. The heart of the fortress is surrounded by several rings of walls and protected by a system of gates, narrow passages and drawbridges. The best-preserved part of the ruins is the East Gatetower which is one of the most interesting examples of Hungarian fortress architecture.

Churches and Chapels

The Catholic parish church in Fő tér is a fine example of Baroque architecture. Higher up on a rock stands a Calvary Chapel of 1770. The Chapel of St Mary on the bank of the Danube was built by followers of Duke Charles of Lorraine in the 18th c.

Surroundings of Visegrád

From Nagyvillám (378 m (1240 ft; hotel) not far from the castle one can look over broad areas of the Pilis range and the Börzsöny Mountains.
There is a footpath from Visegrád to the Pilis Park Forest (Pilisi Parkerdő) with a nature reserve and the wildly romantic Lepence Valley.
Some 6 km (4 miles) from Visegrád lies the village of Dormos near the remains of the well-known Protestant church.

---

*Viziváros

C3–5(M6/7)

Location
District I

Viziváros, the "Water Town" occupies a narrow terrace between Castle Hill and the Danube. Right up until the Turkish

Visegrád
Citadel/Fellegvár

1 East Gate Tower
2 North-west Gate Tower
3 West Gate Tower
4 South-west Gate Tower
5 South Bastion
6 Inner Gate Tower
7 East Palace Range, Chapel
8 Queen's Treasury
9 Treasury Tower
10 Provision Store
11 North Palace Range
12 Matthias Steps
13 Knights' Hall
14 South-west Palace Range

period it was fortified. The Turks set up baths in the part of the town which was chiefly inhabited by fishermen, handworkers and merchants and they turned the existing churches into mosques.

A great deal of building went on in the Baroque Age and this is when, among others, St Anne's Church arose. Since the end of the last century the townscape has altered considerably by the building of several storeyed blocks of flats.

The widening of the Danube led to the sinking of the water-table and as a consequence some of the older buildings subsided and these could only be preserved by means of expensive technology.

HEV Station
Batthyány tér

Underground Station
M2 (Batthyány tér)

Trams
9, 19

Buses
11, 39, 60, 86

*St Anne's Church (Szent Anna-templom)

C4(M6)

St Anne's Church, which was built between 1740 and 1758, to plans by Christoph Hamom and Matthäus Nepauer on a rect-angular plan, is one of the most beautiful Baroque buildings in present-day Hungary. It was painstakingly restored in the 19th c. and again after the Second World War.

The main façade with its two perfectly formed towers is very beautiful. It is decorated with statues by Leonhard Eber and Anton Eberhard. In the centre are St Anne and the Virgin Mary. The civic arms of Buda and a symbol of the Trinity can be seen on the tympanum.

P. C. Molnár and B. Kontuly painted the frescoes on the oval cupola of the nave in 1938. The fresco in the choir, representing the Trinity, was done by G. Vogl in 1772. The High Altar, sur-rounded by pillars and magnificent in its Baroque decoration (St Anne with her daughter Mary in the Temple of Jerusalem) is by K. Bebó who also designed the pulpit.

In the side altars are fine sculptures by Anton Eberhard and splendid paintings by the Viennese artist Franz Wagenschön.

Location
I, south side of Batthyány tér

*Batthyány tér

C4(M6)

This square is named after Count Lajos Batthyány (see Notable Personalities) and has always been the centre of Viziváros. Formerly a market was held here and it is now the terminus of the suburban railway HEV from Szentendre to Budapest and of several bus routes and has an Underground station.

Apart from St Anne's Church there are other notable buildings round the square. The former White Cross Inn (No. 4) was adapted by joining two buildings in 1770. While the right-hand wing reveals Baroque tendencies, the left is Rococo. Behind the arched doorway between the two courtyards a transverse wing was built in the 19th c. Here even theatrical performances and dances could be held. The wrought-iron balustrades on the balconies are also very fine. No. 3, the Hickisch House (Hick-isch-ház), was built in 1795 in the "pigtail" style. The Four Seasons are represented on the reliefs. On the north side of the square stands the former Franciscan monastery (19th c.); in front of it stands a memorial by the artist Ede Kallos honouring the poet who wrote the Hungarian National Anthem.

HEV stop
Batthyány tér

Underground Station
M2 (Batthyány tér)

Trams
9, 19

Buses
11, 39, 60, 86

St Elisabeth's Church (Szent Erzsébet-templom)

C4(M6/7)

This Baroque church, erected in 1757 on the foundations of a Turkish building, originally belonged to the Franciscans. In

Location
I, Fő utca 41–43

View from Castle Hill of Viziváros, Danube and Parliament Building

1785 it was transferred to the Order of Elisabeth which maintained a hospital here, now an old people's home. The statues on the façade of the church and the pulpit fashioned by Franciscan monks are well worth seeing.

*The König Baths (Király-fürdö)   C4

The König Baths have nothing to do with kings. They were the property in the last century of a family named König and are among the most interesting establishments of their kind in Budapest. The oldest part of the buildings, which were severely damaged in the Second World War, is the very well-renovated Hamam (Turkish = bath) built in 1570 under Mustafa Paşa. Its eight-sided main room has a gently curved cupola above it and smaller cupolas ornament the three subsidiary rooms. In the Baroque period the baths were considerably extended and received a beautiful vaulted corridor. In 1827 a Classical wing and a pillared courtyard were added.

Location
I, Fö utca 82–86

St Florian's Chapel (Szent Flórián-kápolna)   C4

This little church is by the architect Matthäus Nepauer (1759/ 60). It is at present used as a local church by adherents of the Greek Catholic faith. On the façade of St Florian's are fine statues of St Nicholas, St Florian and St Blaise. There were once pictures and sculptures by F. Wagenschön, J. Weber and others inside the church but these are now in the Historical Museum on Castle Hill (see entry).

Opposite St Florian's Chapel stands the Hungarian Foreign Ministry (Külügyminisztérium).

Location
I, Fö utca 88

◀ *St Anne's Church in the "Water Town"*

Bem József tér C4

In this square is a monument by J. Istók (1934) commemorating József Bem, a Polish officer who ranged himself in 1848 on the side of the Hungarian freedom fighters. On the plinth of the memorial can be seen works by the lyric poet Sándor Petőfi (see Notable Personalities) who was Bem's Adjutant.

Former Café Friedl C5(M7)

Location
Fő, utca 20

This building, the origins of which go back to the 15th c., was rebuilt in the 18th c. and in 1811 received its neat "pigtail" façade. The corner oriel, crowned by a tower, and the reliefs beneath the windows are very pretty.
The Biedermeier furnishing dates from the middle of the 19th c.

Corvin tér C4/5(M7)

Around Corvin Square, with a fountain by B. Holló (1904), are a number of notable 18th c. building (Nos. 2, 3, 4, and 5). On the south side of the square is the former Capuchin monastery with a church which still shows considerable Turkish influence in its architecture and ornamentation. On the north side stands the former Buda Redoubt, now the headquarters of the Institute of Popular Education and the home of the national art group which has now become quite celebrated.

*Foundry Museum (Öntödei Múzeum) C4

Location
Bem József u. 20

The iron-foundry, built in the middle of the last century by Abraham Ganz, is the core of the industrial complex Ganz (locomotives, wagons, cranes, etc.) which has since become well known far beyond the boundaries of Hungary. The old foundry has quite recently been established as a museum of industrial history.

*Vörösmarty tér D5 (L4)

Location
District V
Underground Station
M1 (Vörösmarty tér)

This square, commemorating the writer Mihály Vörösmarty (see Notable Personalities), lies in the centre of Pest city. The marble monument to the poet was the work of the artists Kallós and Telcs (1908). On the plinth of the memorial twenty-four people are represented, who are reciting Vörösmarty's "Szózat". Round the square are faithfully restored commercial offices. On the west side of the square can be seen the rear of the Cultural Centre (see Vigadó).

Café Gerbeaud

On the north side of Vörösmarty tér can be found the renowned Café Gerbeaud (sometimes known as Café Vörösmarty), which was a popular meeting-place as early as the beginning of this century. A tasteful 19th c. interior and magnificent pastries now attract large numbers of tourists.
This café, which has been famous for a long time, was founded in 1858 by H. Kugler and taken over in 1884 by the Swiss E. Gerbeaud. Under his direction the café and pâtisserie has become well known far beyond the borders of the Hungarian capital.

Vörösmarty Monument in Vörösmarty Square

West Station

See Outer Ring, Marx tér

Ybl Miklós tér

See Tabán

Zichy Castle

See Óbuda

Zoological–Botanical Garden

See City Woodland Park

Zsigmond tér   C3

Zsigmond tér is the most important road junction in the north of Buda. The Trinity Column, set up here in 1733 and which was designed by Ceresola, is worthy of note. The figures on it are by the artists Barbier, Ferretti and Vogl.

Tram
17
Buses
6, 60, 86

Practical Information

Airlines (selection)

Budapest

British Airways, V, Apáczai Cs. J. u. 5, tel. 183–299
Pan American, V, Apáczai Cs. J. u. 4, tel. 187–922
Malév, V, Dorottya u. 2, tel: 189–033, Airport: 572–122

New York

British Airways, 530 Fifth Ave., tel. 1–800–AIRWAYS
Pan American, 600 Fifth Ave., tel. 800–221–1111
Malév, 630 Fifth Ave., tel. 212–757–6480

Airport (repülőtér)

General

Since 1985 the Budapest Ferihegy Airport has had two terminals. At present it can deal with 4 million passengers a year. A
further extension of the airport is possible.

Ferihegy I

Terminal Ferihegy I (16 km/10 miles out from the city centre)
services all foreign airlines and special aircraft (British Airways,
TWA, Pan Am), including the Malév/Air France company.
Malév flights other than Malév/Air France leave from and land
on the ultra-modern Ferihegy II terminal.

Information

General flight information: tel. 577–155 (day and night service).

Ferihegy I information service:
Arrivals and departures tel. 572–122; lost luggage tel. 472–784,
577–690.

Ferihegy II information service:
Arrivals tel. 578–406, 578–477; departures tel. 577–831,
578–768; lost luggage tel. 578–381, 578–108.

Air Terminal (in city centre)

Pest District, V, Engels tér, tel. 186–009.

Getting to and from the
airport

Taxi:
It is relatively expensive to go by taxi from the airport to the city.
There are taxis operated on a cooperative/semi-nationalised
basis (e.g. Fötaxi, Vólantaxi) and also private firms. In any case,
it is advisable to negotiate the fare beforehand.

Hotel buses, shuttle buses:
A number of the first-class hotels run their own bus service.
This service is normally free for guests who have booked into
the hotels concerned.

Airport bus:
Express bus connections every 30 minutes between Ferihegy
terminals I and II and the city centre (Pest) are provided at

reasonable cost by Volán, the national bus company. The single journey takes 30 or 40 minutes.

Underground/municipal bus service.
The cheapest way into the city is by bus and underground. First take the red BKV bus no. 93 as far as the Kőbánya–Kispest terminus of Metro Line 3. It is then just a short trip by underground to the city centre. The return trip is identical.

Antiques

The Bizományi Aruház (BAV) agency advises customers who propose to purchase antiques. The headquarters of BAV is situated in Budapest IX, Kinizsi u. 12, tel: 176–511. Works of art, pictures, carpets and furniture are on sale in various specialist shops. The BAV advises customers about Customs and export regulations.

BAV

Art Exhibitions and Galleries

Adolf Fényes Hall, VII, Rákóczi út 30.
Art Gallery, I, Táncsics Mihály utca 5.
Bertalan Pór Hall, VIII, József körút 70.
Budapest Gallery (Gallery of the Municipal Council), V, Szabadsajitó út 5.
Castle Theatre Gallery (Várszínház) I, Szinház utca 1–3.
Csontváry Terem, V, Vörösmarty tér 1.
Dorottya Gallery, V, Dorottya utca 8.
Ernst Museum, VI, Nagymezö utca 8.
Fészek Gallery, VII, Kertészutca 36.
Gallery of Photographic Art, V, Váci utca 7.
Gyula Derkovits Hall, VI, Lenin körút 63.
Helikon Gallery, V, Eötvös Loránd utca 8.
Imre Varga Exhibition Hall, III, Laktanya utca 8.
István Csók Gallery, V, Váci utca 25 Art Gallery (Mucsarnok), XIV, Hősök tere.

László Paál, VIII, Rákóczi út 57b.
Meta R. Gallery, II, Mártirok útja 8–10.
Mednyánszky Hall, V, Tanács körút 26.
Pest Redoubt (Pesti Vigadó), V, Vigadó tér 2.
Studio Gallery, V, Bajcsy Zsilinszky út 52.

Selection

Banks

The branches of the Hungarian National Bank (MNB) and the State Savings Bank (OTP) are open Mon.–Thurs. 8 a.m.–5 p.m., Fri. 8 a.m.–2 p.m.

Opening times

Branches of the National Bank and Savings Bank as well as authorised bureaux de change exchange money, travellers' cheques and Eurocheques.

Changing money

Baths

See Spas
See Sport

Breakdown Assistance (Auto Repair)

Hungarian Automobile Club (Magyar Autóklub, MAK)	Magyar Autóklub, Rómer Flóris utca 4a, H-1277 Budapest, tel. 152–040 (information service tel. 666–404).
City breakdown service	Autóklub (Yellow Angel), XIV, Francia út 38a, tel. 691–831 and 693–714 (day and night).
Towing service	Volán, Budapest XV, Ifjú Garda utca 117, tel. 409–326. Fösped, Budapest X, Köer utca 3, tel. 475–594, 572–811.
Repair garages	There are some well-equipped repair garages to be found in Budapest and around Lake Balaton. Many hold franchises from foreign manufacturers. You can find the right garage for your car by telephoning the Autóklub on 691–831 and 693–714.

Bus Stations

International Bus Station Engels tér 8	Opening times: daily 5.30 a.m.–9 p.m. Information: general enquiries tel. 182–122; journeys abroad tel. 172–562; journeys within Hungary tel. 172–966 and 172–318. Advance purchase of tickets: daily 5.30 a.m.–7 p.m., tel. 172–345.
Népstadion Bus Station	Opening times: daily 5.30 a.m.–10 p.m. Information: tel. 187–315. Advance purchase of tickets: daily 5.30 p.m.–7 p.m., tel. 187–106.

Cafés, Espressos and Tea Shops

There are very many of these; the ones given here are those which are at present the most popular.

Coffee houses and cafés	Astoria, V, Kossuth L. utca 19 Dunapark, XIII, Poszonyi út 38 *Gerbeaud, V, Vörösmarty tér 7 *Hauer, VII, Rákóczi út 49 Híd, V, Ferenc krt. 15 *Hungária (previously "New York"), VII, Lenin kőrùt. 9–11 Korona, I, Disz tér 6 Különlegességi, VI, Népköztársaság útja 70 Müvész, VI, Népköztársaság útja 29 *Pierrot, Förtuna utca 14 *Ruszwurm, I, Szentháromság utca 7
Espressos	*Angelika, I, Batthyány tér 7 Anna, V, Váci utca 7 Behrám, I, Úri utca 3 Gyöngyszem, IX, Tolbuhin körút 15 Omnia, VIII, Rákóczi út 67 Pálma, VII, Lenin körút 36 Rákóczi, VII, Rákóczi út 40

Szimfónia, IX, Üllői út 65–67
Te + En, II, Bem rakpart 30

Rózsa, VIII, József Kőrút. 31b   Tea shops
Trojka, VI, Népköztársaság útja 28
Bajkal, V, Semmelweis utca 1–3

Camping Sites

The following is a selection.

Magyar Camping és Caravaning Club   Information
H-1085 Budapest, Üllői út 6, tel. 336–536.

Expo Autokemping, X (part of the fair and exhibition area), **Camping sites in the**
Dobi István út 10 (Gate 4), 500 places for tourists, open   **Budapest area**
mid-June–mid-Sept., tel. 778–134.
Caraván, Konkoly utca 18b, open April–Sept.
Hárshegy, II (north-west edge of the city), 320 places, open
Easter–Oct., tel. 151–482.
Métro-Saturnus Tenisz Kemping, XVI (in eastern part of the
city), Csömöri utca 158, 50 places, open Apr.–Oct., tel. 638–
505.
Kemping Üröm, north-west from Budapest, about 80 places,
open mid-Apr.–mid-Oct.
Mini, III (in the north), Vöröshadsereg útja, 40 places, open
May–Sept.
Római Fürdő, III (northern edge of the city), Szentendrei út
189, 1000 places, open all the year round, tel. 887–167.
Tündérhegy, XII (Buda Hills), Szilassy utca 8, 20 places, open
all the year round.
Zugligeti, XII (near the chairlift at Széchenyi hegy, Buda
Hills), Zugligeti út 101, 100 places, open Apr.–mid-Oct.

Vadvirág Kemping, 500 places, open May–Sept., tel. 174.   **Camping site in Esztergom**

Kemping Papsziget, 250 places, open May–Oct.,   **Camping site in Szentendre**
tel. (26) 10–697.

Panoráma Kemping, 800 places, open mid-Apr.–mid-Oct.   **Camping site by Lake Velence**

Kristof Kemping, 40 places, open May–Sept.,   **Camping sites by Lake Balaton**
tel. (86) 38–902.
Mini Kemping, 240 places, open May–Oct.,   Balatonalmádi
tel. (86) 38–906.

Magyar Tenger Kemping, 250 places, open end May–early   Balatonföldvár
Sept., tel. (84) 40–240.

Piroska Kemping, 300 places, open end May–mid-Sept.,   Balatonakarattya
tel. (80) 70–185.

Virius Kemping, 230 places, open mid-May–early Sept.,   Balatonszepezd
tel. (87) 48–048.

Camping Castrum, 200 places, open Apr.–Oct., tel. 12–120.   Keszthely

Car rental

Szántód	Rév Kemping, 200 places, open June–Aug., tel. (84) 31–159.
Tihany/Aszófö	Séd Kemping, 1000 places, open mid-May–mid-Sept., tel. (86) 45–013.
Zamárdi	Autókemping I and II, 1000 places, open May–Sept., tel. (84) 31–163.

Car rental

Hire-centres in Budapest

IBUSZ-Avis
Ferihegy Airport, tel. 475–574
V, Martinelli tér 8, tel. 186–222

Fötaxi Rent-a-car
Ferihegy Airport, tel. 579–123
VII, Kertész utca 24, tel. 116–116

Volán / Europcar National
Ferihegy Airport Terminal 1, tel. 342–540;
Terminal 2, tel. 578–519
IX, Vaskapu utca 16, tel. 334–783

Cooptourist
Ferihegy Airport, tel. 477–328
I, Mészáros utca 56a, tel. 752–058
V, Ferenc körút 43, tel. 131–466

Casino

Budapest Casino

Budapest Hilton Hotel, Hess András tér 1–3, tel: 868–859.
Baccarat, Blackjack, Boule, Roulette, slot machines.
Open: daily from 5 p.m.

Floating Casino

The DDSG casino ship "Schönbrunn", on the Pest bank of the Danube by the Forum Hotel. Roulette, Blackjack, slot machines.
Open daily from spring to beginning of October 2 p.m.–2 a.m.

Héviz Casino

Termál Hotel Héviz. Roulette, Blackjack, slot machines.
Open daily from 5 p.m.

Stakes

Stakes are placed in West German marks. All hard currencies can be exchanged on the spot. Winnings are free of tax and can be freely taken out of Hungary.

Permission to play

Citizens of Socialist countries, except Yugoslavia, are not admitted.

Circus

Municipal Grand Circus

Budapest has its own circus, the Fövárosi Nagycirkusz on the northern edge of the City Woodland Park (Városliget). In the modern circus building, erected in 1971, spectacular performances are given throughout the year (variety, performing animals, etc.).

The Municipal Grand Circus (Fővárosi Nagycirkusz), Allatkerti körút 7, tel: 428–300.

Information and advance booking

Chemists (patika, gyóyszertár)

The address of the nearest chemist can be obtained from the reception desk at every hotel. Although Budapest has a great many chemists it may be difficult to find a particular medicine and it is preferable to bring your own particular medications.

VI, Lenin körút 95, tel. 114–439
VII, Rákóczi út 86, tel. 229–613

Chemists always open

Congress Centre

See A to Z, Congress Centre

Currency

The Hungarian monetary unit is the forint (Ft). One forint=100 fillérs. In circulation are banknotes in denominations of 10, 20, 50, 100, 500 and 1000 forints, coins worth 1, 2, 5, and 10 forints and 10, 20 and 50 fillérs.
Note: The 10 forint and 1000 forint notes are very similar, care should be taken.

Currency

In Hungary, foreigners are not subjected to compulsory exchange of money. According to Hungarian law, foreign currency can only be exchanged at official bureaux de change – at the Hungarian National Bank (MNB), at branches of the Savings Bank (OTP), at travel agencies and tourist offices, at exchange offices in hotels and at camp sites. Changing money privately is strictly forbidden.

Changing money

Exchange rates are subject to fluctuation. The current rates are obtainable from banks, etc.

Exchange rates

In the larger hotels and restaurants and in some shops and stores, American Express, Bank of America, Carte Blanche, Diners Club, Eurocard, Interbanc, Access and Visa credit cards are accepted. Cash may be obtained from banks, bureaux de change, reception desks in the larger hotels and in most tourist offices (IBUSZ, Budapest Tourist, Volán, etc.).

Credit cards

Eurocheques, together with a Eurocheque Card, will be cashed by banks, hotels, boarding-houses, shops and travel agents (e.g. IBUSZ, Budapest Tourist, Volán) who display a Eurocheque sign. In Hungary a Eurocheque must be made out in forints (max. per cheque 10,000 forints). Recipts for cashing the

Eurocheques

141

cheque must be kept, together with the cheque number, until you have left the country.

Currency regulations

Foreigners must declare their currency to the Customs officials. Hungarian currency can only be imported or exported in sums not exceeding 100 forints in coins only. Up to 50 per cent of Hungarian forints which have been exchanged for foreign currency can be exchanged back to a maximum value of $100 US at the following places: the frontier at Hegyeshalom, the Ferihegy Airport in Budapest, IBUSZ offices at the West and East Stations, and IBUSZ offices in the larger hotels.

Customs Regulations

Entry

Articles for use during the holiday (personal effects to be used on the journey, during the stay and to meet weather conditions) can be brought in free of duty. In addition, each person over 16 years of age may bring in 2 litres of wine, 1 litre of spirits, 250 cigarettes, 50 cigars or 250 g of tobacco.
Each traveller may bring in gifts to the value of 10,000 forints. For gifts exceeding this value the Customs duty is 30 per cent.
Sporting guns and ammunition require a special permit.
The import of goods which endanger morals (including pornography and horror films) is prohibited.
Blank video cassettes may be brought into Hungary. There are special regulations relating to the import of video-recorders, walkie-talkies and automatic telephones.

Departure

Articles for use on the journey which have been brought in, may be taken out again without any necessary permit. Food for the journey, but for not more than three days may also be taken out. Tourists who have spent less than three days in Hungary are only allowed food for immediate consumption and not over 100 forints in value.
Gifts to the value of 3,000 forints (no one article to exceed 1,000 forints), but not gold, platinum, silver, museum articles, postage stamps, medicines, carpets, children's shoes, sausage, meat, bacon, sugar, flour and coffee, can be taken out.
Articles which have been bought in the Intertourist shops can be exported but the bill must be produced.

Information

Detailed and Current Customs regulations can be obtained before entry from Hungarian tourist offices or from IBUSZ representatives.

Dentists

Emergency dental treatment (day and night): VII, Maria utca 52, tel. 330–189

Electricity

In the city hotels, apparatus with European plugs can be used. Electricity in Budapest is supplied at 220 volts, 50 cycles AC. Adaptors are necessary for North American type plugs.

Embassies and Consulates (nagykovetseg; konzulatus)

Budapest V, Harmincad u. 6, tel: 182–888	Great Britain
Budapest V, Szabadság tér 12, tel: 126–450	United States
Budapest II, Budakeszi út 32, tel: 767–686	Canada

Emergencies

Important telephone numbers:

tel: 04	Ambulance
tel: 05	Fire
tel: 07	Police
The State health service with all its institutions (district doctors, polyclinics, hospitals and their specialist ambulances) provides free first-aid for tourists. Foreign nationals can obtain out-patient treatment, for which there will be a charge.	Sickness

Events

Spring Festival (concerts, jazz, representational art)	March
Tourist Fair Freedom Festival on the Petőfi tér	15 March
International Fair Book week	May
Theatrum Szentendre	July
Constitution Day; parades, various performances on the Danube, evening firework display on Gellért Hill and on the bank of the Danube	20 August
Budapest Festival (concerts, art exhibitions, theatrical performances, pop) International Fair	September
Museum Month	October

Excursions

Excursions, many with multi-lingual guides, can easily be booked both in Budapest and by Lake Balaton. They will be advertised in travel agents' offices and at hotel reception desks, etc.

To Szentendre by the HEV suburban railway

A trip by yourself by the HEV suburban railway from Batthyány tér to Szentendre (see entry) is very good value for money. This pretty medieval town lies on the edge of the very charming rural area of the Danube Bend (see entry). The trip takes three-quarters of an hour each way.

By cog-wheel railway to Széchenyi Hill

From the valley station near Városmajor Park a cog-wheel railway climbs up this hill (Széchenyi hegy – 439 m/1440 ft high), from where you can go on invigorating walks through the Buda Upland (see entry).

Pioneer Railway

Families with children will enjoy a ride on this railway which is run by young people.

By chairlift to John's Hill

You can go by chairlift from Zugliget up the 529 m/1735 ft high John's Hill. A superb panoramic view can be enjoyed from the observation tower.

Coach excursions

There are plenty of opportunities for getting to know Budapest and the surrounding area by coach. Thanks to the comprehensive public transport network it is quite cheap too.
The most popular and beautiful coach trips on offer include those to the Danube Bend (taking in Szentendre, Visegrád and Esztergom), around Lake Balaton, to Eger (Erlau) and into the Bükk Mountains, as well as to the Hortobágyi Puszta (prairie lands).
Guided tours of the city, with visits to restaurants and wine-tastings, are worth experiencing, as are evening excursions to goulash parties and the "Budapest by Night" tour, which gives you a good insight into the night-life of the "Paris of the East", as Budapest is sometimes known.

By water-bus on the Danube

Local boats (water-buses) ply along the Danube. If you study the time-table carefully you can organise a "Danube cruise" which will enable you to see the most important Budapest landmarks from the river. At weekends "Riverboat Parties" are held on boats equipped with bars.

By hydrofoil or hovercraft to Bratislava or Vienna

If you have the time to spare we would recommend a trip by hydrofoil or hovercraft to Bratislava (Press Castle) or Vienna, incorporating the Danube Bend, one of the most delightful stretches of river in Europe.

See also Sightseeing Programme

Fairs and Exhibitions

Information

Budapesti Nemzetközi Vásár (BNV, Hungexpo), X, Dobó István út 10, tel. 573–555.

Trade Fair Centre

International Trade Fair Centre, Kerepesi út.

Annual Fairs

March

UTAZÁS – International Tourist Fair

Spring

AGROMASEXPO – International Fair for Agriculture and the Food Industry.

HUNGAROPLAST – Fair for the Plastic and Rubber Industry.
LIMEXPO – International Light Industry and Machinery Exhibition.
MIPEL – Exhibition of Electronic and Instrument Construction.

BNV – International Spring Fair (Capital Goods).   May

BNV – International Autumn Fair (Consumer Goods).   September

Multi-annual Fairs

SECUREX – International Fair for Work Safety.
CSINÁLD MAGAD–DO IT YOURSELF – International Exhibition of DIY, Handicrafts and Gardening.
INTERPLAYEXPO – International Toy and Learning Fair.

First-Aid

tel: 04   Emergency

Basic first-aid treatment is free but a charge is made for further   Medical attention
attention. Some doctors have private practices where treatment can be continued with payment.
Visitors should ensure that their insurance provides international cover.

See Chemists

Fishing

Magyar Országos Horgász Szövetség (MOHOSZ), H-1051   Information
Budapest, Október 6 and 20, tel. 325–315.

Folklore

Folklore is very popular in Hungary. You will be hard put to find   Notes
an eating-house or "Csárda" of any size which does not have a gypsy band (in the evenings at least), with all the typical instruments (fiddles, cymbals). At many popular tourists spots you will meet women dressed in traditional Hungarian costume offering rural embroidery and handicrafts for sale. Quite often you may have the chance to take part in a Hungarian wedding celebration or local banquet.

Folklór Centrum, XI, Fehérvári út 47, tel. 452–160.   Folklore centre

The Rajkó Gypsy Orchestra is at present the best ensemble of   Rajkó Gypsy Orchestra
its kind.

Frontier Crossing Points

In spite of the "lifting" of the Iron Curtain in recent months you cannot just enter Hungary as you can a Western country. There are still a limited number of border crossings.

Frontier Crossing Points

Road (open 24 hours a day)

Austria–Hungary	Nickelsdorf–Hegyeshalom Klingenbach–Sopron Rattersdorf–Liebing–Bucsu Deutschkreuz–Kopháza Heiligenkreuz–Rábafüzes
Czechoslovakia–Hungary	Rusovce–Rajka Komarno–Komárom Sahy–Parassapuszta Slovenské Darmoty–Balassagyarmat Slovenské Darmoty–Salgótarján Hranicna pro Hornade–Tornyosnémeti Slovenské Nové Mesto–Sátoraljaújhely
Yugoslavia–Hungary	Hodos–Bajánsenye Dolga Vas–Rédics Gorican–Letenye Terezino Polje–Barcs Donji Miholjac–Drávaszabolcs Knezevo–Udvar Backi Breg–Hercegszántó Kelebia–Tompa Horgos–Röszke Gola–Berzence
Soviet Union–Hungary	Tschop–Záhony
Romania–Hungary	Bors–Artánd Varsand–Gyula Nadlac–Nagylak Petea–Csengersima

Rail (no visas issued)

Austria	Hegyeshalom, Sopron, Szentgotthárd
Czechoslavakia	Komárom, Szob, Hidasnémeti, Rajka, Sátoraljaujhely, Somosköujfalu
Yugoslavia	Kelebia, Gyékényes, Murakeresztur, Magyarboly, Röszke
Soviet Union	Záhony
Romania	Biharkeresztes, Lökösháza, Nyirábrány, Kötegyan

Danube Ships

Budapest, Belgráde rakpart (issue of visas) also (without the issue of visas, only open during daylight): Györ, Komárom, Mohács, Szeged.

Airport

Budapest–Ferihegy I and II (issue of visas)

Food and Drink

Dishes

Hungarian cuisine stresses, as does Austrian, dishes which include meat, flour or cereal, and great attention is paid to spices and other added ingredients. Old recipes which have been handed down are particularly prized and these are characterised by a liberal use of sour cream, lard and spices, especially paprika.

Fresh-water fish (especially carp, catfish and pike-perch) caught in the lakes and numerous ponds is also a great favourite. Most people enjoy a glass of Hungarian wine with their meal; wines from near Lake Balaton are particularly popular.

Some specialities:

Fried veal cutlet (Wiener Schnitzel).	Bécsi szelet
Veal fricassée with rice.	Borjúbecsinált rizzsel
Perch from Lake Balaton.	Fogas
Yeast buns with poppy seeds.	Guba
Well-spiced stew of beef, potato cubes, paprika, onions, tomatoes, garlic and caraway.	Gulyás (Gulasch)
A soup delicately spiced with hot paprika and often consisting of several kinds of fish (carp, catfish, etc.) with the addition of vegetables, onions, croûtons and sour cream.	Halászlé
Soup with liver dumplings.	Halleves majgomboccál
Baked catfish.	Harcsaszeletek roston
Plaited pastry.	Kalács
Layers of vegetables with sausage, bacon, minced meat, potatoes and slices of red pepper.	Koloszvári rakott káposzta
Soup with diced potatoes, croûtons, smoked bacon, tomatoes, slices of red pepper and herbs.	Lebbencs
Slices of red pepper in pork fat, steamed with tomatoes, onions and salt.	Lecsó
White cabbage prepared with a roux and sour cream and added bacon.	Lucskos káposzta

Food and Drink

Mákos metélt	Noodles with poppy seed.
Munkácsy	Eggs in aspic served with a fish salad.
Palacsinta	Pancakes.
Paprikás	Onions, fat, herbs, paprika, meat, tomatoes, strips of red pepper, usually served with dumplings accompanying various meat dishes.
Paprikás csirke galuskával	Chicken with paprika in pastry.
Piroggen	Pastry cases filled with minced meat or finely chopped cabbage and baked.
Pogácsa	Various kinds of pastry.
Pörkölt	Small pieces of meat braised in lard together with onions, paprika, garlic, carroway and marjoram.
Rablóhús nyárson	"Thieves bite" (various pieces of meat, bacon, potato and onion baked on a spit).
Rántott csirke	Fried chicken.
Rétes	Sweet strudel usually filled with apples, nuts, poppy seeds, curd cheese or cherries.
Rigó jancsi	Chocolate cakes with jam.
Somlói galuska	Pieces of biscuit soaked in rum and served with cream.
Tokány	Stewed beef with a thick well-seasoned sauce.
Túróscsusza	Pasta dough with curd cheese and bacon.
Tüzdelt fácánsült	Larded pheasant.
Ujház tyúkleves	Boiling fowl in the Ujhaz manner (with vegetables, onions, garlic, mushrooms, parsley and vermicelli).
Vadas nyúl	Hare, "hunter style".
Zöldbableves	Soup with green beans.
Zöldborsó vajjal	Mange-tout peas prepared with butter.
Zsemlegombóccal	Bread dumplings.

Drinks

Wine (bor)	Wine has traditionally been produced in Hungary since Roman times. The most important Hungarian vineyards are in Sopron,

Mór, Balaton, Eger, Tokaj, Szekszárd, Pecs, Vilány and Szeged. Their products can be sampled in numerous Budapest inns.

Favourite white wines:
Veltlini (Veltliner), Muskateli (Muscatel), Tramini (Traminer), Olazrizling (Italian Riesling), Rizling (Riesling), Szilváni (Silvaner), Szürkebarát (Grey Monk or Ruländer) and Furmint.

Popular red wines:
Bikavér ("Bull's Blood"), Kékfrankos (Blue Frankish), Leányka, Cabernet, Pinot Noir, Merlot.

Rosé wine:
Kadarka.

The wine label:
fehér=white; vörös=red; száras=dry; habzó=sparkling; édes=sweet;
kimert bor=vin ordinaire; asztali bor=table wine; minösegi bor=quality wine.

Tokaji Wine:
The Furmint grape and the Hárslevelü grape ripen very well in the region around Tokaj. The fruits are also affected by "noble rot", which adds appreciably to the sugar-content and taste. Tokaji is produced in three qualities: furmint (dry and light), szamorodni (mild and sweet), aszu (late vintage; with three, four or five stars; only in limited quantity).

Hungarian fruit brandies are famous and popular, especially Barack (apricot brandy), Szilva (plum brandy) and, last but not least, cherry brandy.

Spirits

As well as local beers, Yugoslavian and Austrian beers are becoming more and more popular in Budapest.
Connoisseurs of beer appreciate the Wernesgrüner, fresh from the barrel, which is imported from East Germany and is available in some inns.

Beer (sor)

Getting to Budapest

There are scheduled flights daily by British Airways and Malév from London to Budapest, either direct or via Rome or Frankfurt. From the USA and Canada visitors normally fly to Amsterdam, Copenhagen, Paris, Madrid or Vienna and continue on connecting flights to Budapest.

By air

The best service from the UK leaves Victoria Station in the morning and arrives at Budapest the following afternoon, via Dover, Ostend and Vienna. It is possible to change in Paris and continue on the Orient Express. An alternative route is via the Hook of Holland and Vienna.

By rail

Visitors taking their cars to Hungary are advised to travel on the German autobahns between Cologne and Munich to Salzburg and from there to Budapest. The AA in Great Britain and the AAA in the United States can provide further information.

By road

Gliding

By boat | During the summer (May–September) there is a hydrofoil service on the Danube between Vienna, Bratislava and Budapest, the journey taking between four and five hours.

Gliding

Gliding Club | Budapest Flying Club (Mezőgasági Repülök Klubja)
Sponsor: Budapest Technical University

Gliding airfield | Hármashatár-hegy (about 6 km (4 miles) north-west of the city centre).

Golf

Kisoroszi golf course | The newly laid out Kisoroszi golf course (18 holes) is on an island of the Danube 38 km (24 miles) north of the city centre. Information about using the course can be obtained from the reception desk at the Budapest Hilton Hotel.

Horse-drawn Cabs (Fiacres)

In Buda and in Pest horse-drawn cabs have operated since the 18th c., just as in Vienna. After suffering from increasing competition from taxis, they have reappeared, especially in the castle quarter, as a tourist attraction.

Hospital

Important general hospitals | István kórház
IX, Nagyvárad tér 1, tel: 340–350

János kórház
XII, Diós árok 1, tel: 154–030

Margit kórház
III, Bécsi út 132, tel: 687–420

Semmelweis kórház
VIII, Gyulai Pál u. 2, tel: 342–180

Rescue Service Hospital
VI, Szobi u. 3, tel: 119–850

University Clinic
Üllői út, tel: 135–216

Hotels (selection)

Categories | Hungarian hotels are divided into five categories (1–5 stars). The 4- and 5-star hotels offer the same degree of comfort and

Inside Hotel Atrium Hyatt

service as luxury hotels of the same standard in Western countries. The 2- and 3-star hotels provide an acceptable standard and those with one-star should be considered as simple tourist hotels.

Prior reservation is recommended. This is particularly so at the time of the Spring Festival, the Easter and Whitsun holidays, Ascension Day and the Feast of Corpus Christi, as well as during the summer and autumn holidays. Hotel rooms in Hungary can be reserved at any good travel agent. **Reservations**

Reservation offices in Budapest:
Danubius Travel, V, Martinelli tér 8, tel. 173–652.
Hungar Hotels Service, V, Petőfi Sándor utca 14, tel. 183–018.
IBUSZ Hotel Service, V, Petőfi tér 3, tel. 185–707 (day and night).

These can be obtained free of charge from Tourinform, Süto utca 2 (Pest district, near Deák tér, open daily 8 a.m.–8 p.m.), tel. 179–800. **Hotel catalogues/brochures**

Prices of hotels in Hungary range from about £8/$16 per night for a single room in a 1-star hotel to over £170/$340 for a suite in a 5-star hotel. Hotels some way outside Budapest are noticeably cheaper than those of similar standard in the city. **Prices**

Hotels in Budapest

The Roman numeral after the name of the hotel denotes the district in which the hotel stands; ''r''= ''rooms''. **Note**

Hotels

*****   Atrium Hyatt, V, Roosevelt tér 2, tel. 383–000, 351 r.
Duna Inter-Continental, V, Apáczai Csere János utca 4, tel. 175–122, 340 r.
Hilton Budapest, I, Hess András tér 1–3, tel. 751–000, 323 r.
Thermál, XIII, Margit–sziget, tel. 321–100, 206 r.

****   Béke-Radisson, VI, Lenin körút 97, tel. 323–300, 238 r.
Buda-Penta, I, Krisztina körút 41–43, tel. 566–333, 395 r.
Flamenco, XI, Tass vezér utca 7, tel. 252–250, 360 r.
Fórum, V, Apáczai Csere János utca 12–14, tel. 178–088, 400 r.
Gellért, XI, Szent Gellért tér 1, tel. 852–200, 235 r.
Grand Hotel Hungária, VII, Rákóczi út 90, tel. 229–050, 528 r.
Grand Hotel Royal, VII, Lenin körút 47–49, tel. 533–133, 366 r.
Nemzeti, VIII, József körút 4, tel. 339–160, 50 r.
Novotel Budapest, XII, Alkotás utca 63–67, tel. 869–588, 324 r.
Ramada, XIII, Margitsziget, tel. 111–000, 163 r.

***   Aero, IX, Ferde utca 1–3, tel. 274–690, 139 r.
Astoria, V, Kossuth Lajos utca 19, tel. 173–411, 130 r.
Austrotel Palace, VIII, Rákóczi út 43, tel. 136–000, 113 r.
Budapest, II, Szilágyi Erzsébet fasor 47, tel. 153–230, 280 r.
Emke, VII, Akácfa utca 1–3, tel. 229–230, 70 r.
Erzsébet, V, Károlyi Mihály utca 11–15, tel. 382–111, 123 r.
Expo, X, Dobi 1 and 10, tel. 842–130, 160 r.
Orion, I, Döbrentei utca 13, tel. 568–933, 32 r.
Rege, II, Pálos út 2, tel. 767–311, 80 r.
Stadion, XIV, Ifjúság utca 1–3, tel. 631–830, 382 r.
Taverna, V, Váci utca 20, tel. 384–999, 224 r.
Thermál Hotel Aquincum, XIII, Margitsziget, tel. 321–100, 312 r.
Volga, XIII, Dozsa Gy. út 65, tel. 290–200, 306 r.

**   Ifjúság, II, Zivatar utca 1–3, tel. 353–331, 100 r.
Metropol, VII, Rákóczi út 58, tel. 421–175, 102 r.
Park, VIII, Baross tér 10, tel. 131–420, 173 r.
Vénusz, III, Dósa utca 2–4, tel. 687–252, 73 r.
Vörös Csillag, XII, Rege út 21, tel. 750–522, 40 r.
Wien (Vienna), XI, Budaörsi út 88–90, tel. 665–400, 110 r.

*   Citadella, XI, Gellérthegy, Citadella sétány, tel. 665–794, 30 r.
Express, XII, Beethoven utca 7–9, tel. 752–082, 22 r.

Hotels on the Danube Bend

Esztergom   ***Esztergom, Primás-sziget, Nagy Duna sétány, tel. 81–68, 377 r.
**Fürdő, Bajcsy-Zsilinszky utca 14, tel. 292

Szentendre   **Danubius, Ady E. utca 28, tel (26) 12–511
**Hubertusz, Tyúkus-dűlőutca 10, tel. (26) 10–616.
*Sziget, Papsziget, tel. (26) 10–697.

Vác   Pension Tabán, Korvin lépcső 3, tel. (27) 11–607.

Visegrád   ***Silvanus, Fekete-hegy, tel. 136–063, 80 r.
**Vár, Fő utca 9–11, tel. (26) 28–264.

Hotels by Lake Balaton

Note   Most of the hotels by Lake Balaton are normally open May–Sept.

Pension Harsona, Szegedi Róza utca 37, tel. (87) 31–227.   Badacsony

***Aurora, Bajcsy-Zsilinszky utca 14, tel. (86) 38–811, 240 r.   Balatonalmádi
*Tulipán, Marx tér 1, tel. (86) 38–317.

***Neptun, Park, tel. (84) 40–388, 200 r.   Balatonföldvár
**Fesztivál, Rákóczi utca 40, tel. (84) 40–377

***Annabella, Beloiannisz utca 25, tel. (86) 42–222, 391 r.   Balatonfüred
***Margaréta, Széchenyi út 29, tel. (86) 43–824, 52 r.
***Marina, Széchenyi utca 26, tel. (86) 43–644, 375 r.

Platán, Hunyadi utca 56, tel. (84) 50–203.   Boglárielle

****Aqua, Kossuth Lajos utca 13–15, tel. 11–090, 213 r.   Hévíz
***Thermál, Kossuth Lajos utca 9–11, tel. 11–190, 203 r.
**Napsugár, Tavirósza utca 3–5, tel. 13–208.

***Helikon, Balatonpart 5, tel. 11–330, 232 r.   Keszthely
**Phoenix, Balatonpart, tel. 12–630.
Amazon, Szabadság út 11, tel. 12–448.

***Balaton, Petöfi sétany 9, tel. (84) 10–655, 137 r.   Siófok
***Európa, Petöfi sétany 15, tel. (84) 13–411, 150 r.
***Hungária, Petöfi sétany 13, tel. (84) 10–677, 140 r.
***Lido, Petöfi sétany 11, tel. (84) 10–633, 137 r.
**Napfény, Mártirok utca 8, tel. (84) 11–408, 57 r.
**OKGT, Beszédes József sétany, tel. (84) 11–633.
**Vénusz, Kinizsi utca 12, tel. (84) 10–660.
*Touring, Foki-hegy, tel. (84) 10–684.

****Club Tihany, Rev utca, tel. (86) 48–088, 161 r.   Tihany

Information

See Tourist Information

Language

Visitors will have little difficulty in making themselves under-   Foreign languages
stood in Budapest, for a knowledge of foreign languages is a
traditional part of general education, especially as Hungarian
is a language which is understood by relatively few non-
Hungarians and does not figure among the recognised
international languages. German is widely understood in Hungary and many young people also speak quite good English.

Hungarian belongs to the Finno-Ugrian family and therefore   Hungarian
has a special place in Europe. The varying pronunciation of
consonants and vowels will cause difficulty for the uninitiated.
In Hungarian the first syllable is the one always stressed.

Language

The alphabet and its
pronunciation

Approximate equivalent in English
a=short open o (as in hot)
á=long a (as in calm)
c=ts (as in bits)
cs=ch (as in chat)
e=short e (as in bet)
é=long e (as the ai in fair)
gy⌒i (as adieu in French)
i=short i (as in bit)
í=long i (as the ee in breeze)
ly=sound of a voiced y (as in yes)
ny=gn (as in Cognac)
o=short o (as in cot)
ó=long o (as in mow)
ö=short o (as the e in the)
ő=long o (as the u in fur)
s=sh (as in show)
sz=sharp z (as in purse)
ty=ty (as the ch in chance)
u=short u (as in butter)
ú=long u (as the oo in boot)
ü=short u (as in hue)
ű=long u (as in French tu)
v=v (as in very)
z=voiced z (as in buzz)
zs=voiced j (as in judge)

Numbers

0	null, zéró, semmi	11	tizenegy	100	száz
1	egy	12	tizenkettő	200	kétszáz
2	kettő, két	20	húsz	1000	ezer
3	három	21	huszonegy		
4	négy	30	harminc		
5	öt	40	negyven		
6	hat	50	ötven		
7	hét	60	hatvan		
8	nyolc	70	hetven		
9	kilenc	80	nyolcvan		
10	tiz	90	kilencven		

Days of the week

Monday	hétfő	Friday	péntek
Tuesday	kedd	Saturday	szombat
Wednesday	szerda	Sunday	vasárnap
Thursday	csütörtök	Holiday	ünnep

Important words and
phrases

accommodation	szállas
address	cim
airport	repülőgép
autumn	ősz
bed	ágy
bill	számla
blue	kék
boat	csónak
bread	kenyér
bridge	hid
café	kávéház
castle	kastély
closed	zárva
day	nap
departure	indulás
diversion	terelőút

doctor	orvos
door	ajtó
early closing day	szimnap
east	kelet
embassy (consulate)	követség
emergency exit	vészkijárat
entrance	bejárat
evening	este
exchange	pénzváltás
exit	kijárat
express train	gyorsvonat
filling station	benzinkút
first-aid	elsősegély
free	szabad
frontier	határ
German	németül
Good bye	viszontlatasra
Good day	jó napot
Good evening	jó estét
Good morning	jó reggelt
help, assistance	segitség
hill	domb
hour, clock	óra
How much?	mennyi?
How much is that?	mennyibe kerül?
Hungary	Magyarország
I (don't) understand	(nem) értem
information	információ, felvilágositás
inn	vendéglő
island	sziget
lake, pond	tó
left	balra
letter	lévél
look out!	vigyázat!
luggage	poggyász
Madam (addressing a lady)	asszony
May I?	megengedi?
milk	tej
name	név
night	éjszaka
no parking	várakozni tilos!
north	észak
pardon	pardon!
pâtisserie	cukrászada
play street	játszóutca
please	kérem
police	rendőrség
post office	Posta
prohibited	tilos!
railway	vasút
red	piros
restaurant	etterem
right	jobbra
road, street	utca, út
road works	útjavitás
room	szoba
shop, store	aruház
Sir (addressing a gentleman)	úr
south	dél
spring	tavasz

Lost property Offices

station	állomás, pályaudvár
storey	emelet
summer	nyár
telegram	távirat
Thank you	köszönöm
tip	borravaló
toilet (gentlemen)	urak
toilet (ladies)	nők
town	város
tram	villamos
water	víz
weather	idöjárás
week	hét
west	nyugat
What is that?	mi ez?
When?	mikor?
Where?	hol?
white	fehér
wine bar	borozó
wine vault	borpince
winter	tél
village	falu
year	év
yellow	sárga
yesterday	tegnap

Lost property Offices (talált tárgyak osztálya)

Foreigners' Department KÉA	VI, Rudas László utca 45. Mon. 8.30 a.m.–4.30 p.m., Tues.–Fri. 8.30 a.m.–12 noon.
Fötaxi, City-Taxi, Radio-Taxi Buda-Taxi, Taxiunion	Central Lost Property Office, V, Engels tér, tel. 174–961. Mon.–Thur. 8 a.m.–4.30 p.m., Fri. 8 a.m.–4 p.m.
Volántaxi	XIV, Jerney utca 56–58, tel. 637–000. Mon.–Fri. 6 a.m.–7 p.m.
Budapest Transport Services (BKV)	VII, Akácfa utca 18, tel. 226–613. Mon.–Fri. 7.30 a.m.–3.30 p.m.
MAHART	V, Belgrád rakpart (ship mooring). Open by arrangement; tel. 181–704.
South Railway Station	Tel. 759–485.
West Railway Station	Tel. 490–115.
East Railway Station	Tel. 225–615.
Ferihegy Airport	Terminal I: tel. 472–484. Terminal II: tel. 578–108.

Museums

Opening times	Budapest museums are generally open Tues.–Sun. between 10 a.m. and 6 p.m.

Museum complex in Castle Palace

Roman remains on Danube bank

Museums

Entrance fee

Most museums make an entrance charge, the amount of which varies depending on how attractive the exhibits are. In many museums admission is free on Saturdays.

List of museums

Agricultural Museum (Mezógazdasági Múzeum)
See A–Z, City Woodland Park

Art Gallery (Műcsarnok)
See A–Z, Heroes' Square

Arts and Crafts Museum (Iparművészeti Múzeum)
See A–Z, Arts and Crafts Museum

Aquincum (Archaeological Museum)
See A–Z, Óbuda

Béla Bartók House (Bartók Béla Emlekház)
II, Csalán u. 29

Castle Museum, Historical Museum (Történeti Múzeum)
See A–Z, Castle Palace

Castle Museum Nagytétény (Nagytétény Kastély-múzeum)
See A–Z, Nagytétény

China Museum (Kina-múzeum)
See A–Z, China Museum

Church Museum (Matthias Church)
See A–Z, Matthias Church

Commerce and Catering Museum
(Kereskedelmi és Vendéglátóipari Múzeum)
See A–Z, Buda, Important Streets and Squares, Fortuna utca

Contra Aquincum
See A–Z, Március 15 tér

Entre-Ady Memorial
V, Veres Pálné utca 4–6

Ernst Museum (Ernst Múzeum)
See A–Z, Nagymező utca

Ethnographical Museum (Néprajzi Múzeum)
See A–Z, Ethnographical Museum

Evangelical Provincial Museum
(Evangélikus Országos Múzeum)
See A–Z, Inner Ring, Deák Ferenc tér

Ferenc Hopp Museum for East Asian Art
(Hopp Ferenc Kelet-ázsiai Művészeti Múzeum)
See A–Z, Ferenc Hopp Museum for East Asian Art

Fire Brigade Museum (Tűzoltó-múzeum)
See A–Z, Kőbánya

Foundry Museum (Öntödei Múzeum)
See A–Z, Víziváros

Franz Liszt Museum
VI, Vörösmarty utca 35

Gizi Bajor Theatre Museum
XII, Stromfeld Aurél utca 16; open Tues., Thur. 3 p.m.–6 p.m.,
Sat., Sun. 10 a.m.–6 p.m.

Gül Baba Türbe
II, Mecset utca 14; open Apr.–Oct. daily 10 a.m.–6 p.m., Nov.–
Mar. daily 10 a.m.–2 p.m.

Hercules Villa
III, Meggyfa utca 18–20; open Apr.–Oct. Tues.–Fri. 10 a.m.–
2 p.m., Sat., Sun. 10 a.m.–6 p.m.

Historical Museum
See A to Z, Castle Palace

Jewish Museum
(Országos Zsidó Vallási és Történeti Gyűjtemény)
See A–Z, Pester Synagogue

Jewish Rural Museum
Synagoge Dohány utca 2; open Apr.–Oct. Mon., Thur. 2 p.m.–
6 p.m., Tues., Fri. 10 a.m.–1 p.m.

József Attila Museum
IX, Gát utca 3

Kiscelli Museum (Kiscelli Múzeum)
See A–Z, Óbuda

Kodály Museum
VI, Népköztársaság útja
Mementos of the composer: archives

Local History Museum Óbuda
(Óbuda Helytörténeti Múzeum)
III, Fű tér

Military History Museum (Hadtörténeti Múzeum)
See A–Z, Buda, Important Streets and Squares,
Kapisztrán tér

Molnár Collection
XI, Ménesi út 65; open Tues.–Thur. daily 3 p.m.–6 p.m., Sun.
10 a.m.–1 p.m.

Mór Jókai Museum
XII, Költő utca 21; open Tues.–Sun. 10 a.m.–2 p.m.

Museum of Fine Arts (Szépművészeti Múzeum)
See A–Z, Museum of Fine Arts

Museum of the Hungarian Workers' Movement
(Magyar Munkásmozgalmi Múzeum)
See A–Z, Castle Palace

Musical History Museum of the Hungarian Academy of Science
I, Tancsics Mihaly utca 7; open Mon. 4 p.m.–9 p.m., Wed.–Sun.
10 a.m.–6 p.m.

National Gallery (Nemzeti Galéria)
See A–Z, Castle Palace

National Museum (Nemzeti Múzeum)
See A–Z, National Museum

Natural History Museum
(Természettudományi Múzeum)
VIII, Baross u. 13

Open Air Museum Szentendre (Skanzen)
See A–Z, Szentendre

Petőfi Museum (Petőfi Múzeum)
See A–Z, Petőfi Museum

Pharmaceutical Museum "Golden Eagle"
(Arany Sas Patika-múzeum)
See A–Z, Buda, Important Streets and Squares,
Tárnok utca

Physical Education Museum
XIV, Dózsa György út 3

Postage Stamp Museum (Bélyeg-múzeum)
VII, Hársfa utca 47

Postal Museum (Posta Múzeum)
See A–Z, Népköztarsaság útja

Roman Military Baths
III, Flórián tér 4–5; open Apr.–Oct. Tues.–Fri. 10 a.m.–2 p.m.,
Sat., Sun. 10 a.m.–6 p.m.

Roman Military Town (Táborvárosi Múzeum)
See A–Z, Óbuda

Semmelweis Museum (Semmelweis Múzeum)
See A–Z, Tabán

Sport Museum
XIV, Dózsa György út 3

Transport Museum (Közlekedési Múzeum)
See A–Z, City Woodland Park

Underground Railway Museum (Földalatti Vasúti Múzeum)
See A–Z, Inner Ring, Deák Ferenc tér

Music

Franz List Academy of Music
VI, Liszt Ferenc tér 8

Concert halls

Vigadó
V, Vigadó tér

Buda Redoubt
I, Corvin tér 8

Matthias Church
I, Szentharomság tér

Reformed Church
V, Kálvin tér

Zichy Castle
II, Fő tér 1

State Opera House
VI, Nepköztársaság útja 22

Opera

Tourist Information, tel: 179–800

Programme of events

Philharmonia,
V Vörösmarty tér 1
tel: 176–222

Advance booking

Naturism

Delegyhaza Naturist Camp (30 km (19 miles) south of Budapest)

Delegyhaza

Szuyogsziget Naturist Area

Lake Velence

Balatonbéreny near Keszthely
(section of beach)

South-west bank of Lake Balaton

Newspapers and Magazines

It is possible to buy some Western newspapers and magazines in shops and in the major hotels. The newspapers *The Times*, *The International Herald Tribune* (Paris edition) and the weekly *Time* and *Newsweek* magazines are available the day after their publication.

International press

Night-life

English-language
publications

A bilingual English-German paper, *The Daily News – Neueste Nachrichten*, is published by the Hungarian news agency MTI and is widely available. There is also a free monthly magazine *Coming Events in Hungary* also with text in English and German and additionally in French. A new Hungarian quarterly in English deals with Hungarian life, culture and politics.

Night-life

General

As regards its night-life, too, Budapest has earned its reputation as the "Paris of the East". A wide spectrum of entertainments, ranging from serious symphony concerts and classical drama to adventurous modern plays offers something to meet all tastes. Gypsy bands and folk-groups perform in many eating-houses in the evenings, and in many better-class nightspots you can enjoy some exciting revues or variety programmes and cabaret. Jazz clubs, night-clubs and numerous discos stay open until the early hours.

Night-clubs (selection)

Casanova, I, Batthyány tér 4, tel. 338–320.
Horoszkóp, VII, Krisztina körút 41–43, tel. 566–333.
Lido (Belvárosi Kávéház Lido), V (Pest), Szabadsajtó utca 5, tel. 182–404.
Maxim, VII, Akácfa utca 3, tel. 227–858.
Moulin Rouge, VI, Nagymező utca 17, tel. 124–492.
Pipacs-Bár, V, Aranykéz utca 15, tel. 185–759.
Orfeusz, VI, Lenin körút 97, tel. 323–300.

Discos (selection)

Atrium Hyatt Star Laser Disco, V (Pest), Roosevelt tér 2, tel. 383–000.
Fekete Macska, IX, Knézits utca 1, tel. 170–469.
Fortuna, I, Hess András tér 4, tel. 7752–401.
Novotel Disco Mediterran, XII, Alkotás utca 63–67, tel. 668–007.
Ördögoro Csárda, XII, Edvi Illés utca, tel. 251–449.
Randevú, XII, Lékai J. tér 9, tel. 850–986.
Római To, III, Rozgonyi Piroska utca 2, tel. 689–529.
Skála Métro Disco, VI, Marx tér 1–2, tel. 322–162.

Opening times

Food shops

Mon.–Fri. 7 a.m.–7 p.m., Sat. 7 a.m.–2 p.m. Some food shops also open on Sunday mornings.

Stores (with no food
department)

Mon., Tue., Wed. and Fri. 10 a.m–6 p.m., Thur. 10 a.m.–8 p.m., Sat. 9 a.m.–1 p.m.

Banks

Mon.–Thurs. 8 a.m.–5 p.m., Fri. 8 a.m.–2 p.m.

Post offices

Mon.–Fri. 8 a.m.–7 p.m., Sat. 8 a.m.–12 noon.

Museums

Usually Tues.–Sun. 10 a.m.–6 p.m.

Hairdressers

Mon.–Fri. 7 a.m.–9 p.m., Sat. 7 a.m.–4 p.m.

Opera

See Music
See Theatre

Photography (fénykép)

Photographing and filming military and industrial areas, air-ports, railway stations, bridges and radio stations is forbidden. In frontier areas and shops there is an absolute ban on photography.

Prohibited

Except for the information given above anything in Hungary may be photographed and filmed for private use.
Photographs and films intended for commercial use must be declared to the Pressinform Office.
Permission from the appropriate authority should be sought before photographing industrial, agricultural or administrative installations. An individual's permission should be obtained before he or she is photographed.

Permitted

It is advisable to bring films, etc. in sufficient quantity with you since Western miniature and super-8 films can only be obtained in a few shops.

Film material

Police (Rendőrseg)

Tel. 07

Emergency

Aliens Department of the Chief Police Commissariat (KÉA), VI, Népköztársaság útja 12, tel. 115–889, 118–668.
Opening times: Mon. 8 a.m.–5 p.m., Tue.–Fri. 9 a.m.–12 noon, all day on Sat., Sun. and public holidays.

Alien authorities KÉA (Police dealing with foreigners)

Post (posta)

V, Petőfi Sándor utca 13–15
Opening times: Mon.–Sat. 7 a.m.–9 p.m., Sun. and holidays 8 a.m.–1 p.m.

Main Post Office

Keleti pályaudvar (East Station)
VIII, Baross tér 11/c

Post offices open 24 hours a day

Nyugati pályaudvar (West Station)
VI, Lenin körút 105

Magyar Posta (Main Post Office)
H-1052 Budapest
V, Petőfi Sándor utca 13–15

Poste restante

Annexe of Main Post Office
V, Petőfi Sándor utca 17–19
Opening times: Mon.–Sat. 7 a.m.–9 p.m., Sun. and holidays 8 a.m.– 1 p.m.

Long-distance Telephone, Telegrams, Telex

Private Rooms

Telegrams by phone	tel: 02
Telephone	See Telephone

Private Rooms

	In Budapest and around Lake Balaton it is often possible to find rooms to let privately at favourable rates. Skill in negotiating terms will be a distinct advantage.
Finding rooms to let	In Budapest, consult: Budapest Tourist, V, Roosevelt tér 5, tel. 173–555. IBUSZ, V, Petőfi tér 3, tel. 185–707. Volántourist, V, Belgrád rakpart 6, tel. 182–133.
	In the area around Lake Balaton and in the larger places on the Danube Bend you should try the local travel bureaux (IBUSZ, Volán, COOP, Express, etc.).

Public Holidays

1 January	New Year
15 March	Commemoration Day of Struggle for Freedom 1848
4 April	Liberation Day
March/April	Easter Monday
1 May	Labour Day
20 August	Constitution Day
7 November	Anniversary of the Great October Socialist Revolution
25–26 December	Christmas

Public Transport

Times of local public transport	Public transport in Budapest is provided by trams, trolley-buses, buses and the underground (Metro). Trams, trolley-buses and the underground generally operate between 4 a.m. and midnight, buses between 5 a.m. and 11 p.m. Some routes run night and day.
Tickets for buses and trams	Tickets for trams and buses can be obtained in advance from hotels, tobacconists, travel agents and special vending machines. No tickets can be bought on the vehicles. Tickets are only valid for one journey and have to be cancelled by the passenger in a machine on the vehicle.
Underground	To travel on the underground the passenger has to insert a one forint coin at the station entrance.

A Budapest tram   *Excursion, ship on the Danube*

The Budapest Transport Authority sells separate tickets of vari- All-day tickets
ous values enabling you to travel as far as you like on buses and
underground trains.

The cog-wheel railway on the Szabadság-hegy, the chair-lift on Rail
the János-hegy, the funicular on Castle Hill and the local boats
on the Danube are also under the control of the Budapest
Transport Authority.

Radio (Magyar Rádió és Televizió, MRT)

There are brief bulletins in English broadcast on Budapest
radio and TV. There are two television channels and on Channel 2 imported programmes can sometimes be seen, either in
the original language or with English sub-titles.

Railways (Hungarian State Railways: MÁV)

MÁV Central Information Office, open daily 6 a.m.–9 p.m. Information

Travelling to other countries; tel. 224–052. Travel information by
Travelling within Hungary: tel. 227–860, 429–150. telephone

VI, Népköztársaság útja 35, tel. 228–049, 228–056. MÁV Customer Service

Restaurants (selection)

MÁVTOURS

VI, Népköztársaság útja 35, tel. 228–049.
XII, Déli pályaudvar (South Station), tel. 759–485.

Lost property

Suitcases and other property lost on trains should be reported as soon as possible to the railway station to which you are travelling.

Railway stations

East Station (Keleti pályaudvar)

Train information: tel. 136–835.
Trains to Austria, Switzerland, West Germany, France, Belgium and Holland, as well as to Czechoslovakia and East Germany.
Internal traffic to Miskolc and Békéscsaba.

South Station (Déli pályaudvar)

Train information: tel. 558–657.
Trains to Austria and Yugoslavia.
Regional trains to Lake Velence and Lake Balaton, and to Pécs, Tapolca, Szombathely and Győr.

West Station (Nyugati pályaudvar)

Train information: tel. 490–115.
Trains to Czechoslovakia and East Germany.
Internal traffic to Debrecen and Szeged.

Travelling to Hungary by train

See Getting to Budapest.

Restaurants (selection)

Note

Hot meals are obtainable until quite late where indicated. On the days named the restaurants are usually closed. In many restaurants there is gypsy or Viennese music in the evenings.

International cuisine

*Alabárdos, I, Országház utca 2, tel. 560–851.
*Apostolok, V, Kigyó utca 4–6, tel. 183–704, until midnight.
Bolero (in the Flamenco Hotel), XI, Tass vezér utca 7, until 11.30 p.m., tel. 612–150
Budavár (in the Buda Penta Hotel), I, Krisztina körút 41–43, tel. 566–333, until midnight.
Csárda (in the Duna Inter-Continental Hotel), V, Apáczai Csere J. utca 4, tel. 175–122, until midnight.
Duna (in the Gellért Hotel), XI, Szent Gellért tér 1, tel. 852–200, until midnight.
Dunacorsó, V, Vigadó tér 3, tel. 186–362.
Evergreen (Olympia Hotel), XII, Eötvös út 40, tel. 568–011, until 11 p.m.
*Gundel, XIV, Állatkerti körút 2, tel. 213–550, noon–4 p.m. and 7 p.m.–midnight.
Halászbástya, I, Hess András tér 1–3, tel. 561–446, until midnight.
Hársfa, II, Vörös Hadsereg útja 132, tel. 350–997.
Hungária, VII, Lenin körút 9–11, tel. 223–849, until 10 p.m.
Kalocsa (in the Hilton Hotel), I, Hess András tér 1–3, tel. 751–000, until midnight.
Karolina (in the Novotel Hotel), XII, Alkotás út 63–67, tel. 869–588, until midnight.
Légrádi, V, Magyar utca 23, ,tel. 186–804.
Mátyás Pince, V, Március tér 7, tel. 181–650, until 1 a.m.

Restaurant with Gipsy music

Paksi Halszcsárda, II, Mártirok útja 14, tel. 358–389, until midnight.
Oldtimer (in the Atrium Hyatt Hotel), V, Roosevelt tér 2, tel. 383–000, until midnight.
Paradiso, XII, Istenhegyi út 40a, tel. 561–988.
Platán (in the Thermál Hotel), XIII, Margitsziget, tel. 321–100, until midnight.
Silhouette (in the Forum Hotel), V, Apáczai Csere J. utca 12, tel. 178–088.
Szondy (in the Béke Radisson Hotel), VI, Lenin körút 97, tel. 323–300, until midnight.
Tokaj (in the Atrium Hyatt Hotel), V, Roosevelt tér 2, tel. 383–000.
Százéves, V, Pesti Barnabás utca 2, tel. 183–608.
Vadrósa, II, Pentelei Molnár utca 15, tel. 351–118.

Aranyszarvas I, Szarvas tér 1, tel. 756–451, until 1 a.m. (game).

Specialty restaurants

Bajkál, V, Semmelweiss utca 1–3, tel. 176–839 (specialities from the Soviet Union).
Berlin City Hall Cellar Restaurant, VII, Dob utca 31, tel. 773–674, until 11 p.m.
Bukarest, XI, Bartók Béla út 48, tel. 666–580, until 5 a.m. (Romanian cuisine).
Dunapark, XIII, Pozsonyi út 38, tel. 295–620 (esp. fish and game dishes).
Etoile, XIII, Pozsonyi út 4, tel. 122–242, until midnight (French cuisine).
Fehér Galamb, I, Szentháromság tér 9–11, tel. 756–975, until midnight.

Restaurants (selection)

Habana, VI, Bajcsy-Zsilinszky út 21, tel. 121–039, until 3 a.m. (Cuban-Creole cuisine),
Hanna, VII, Dob utca 35, tel. 427–359, (Kosher cuisine).
Japán, VIII, Luther utca 4–6, tel. 143–427, (Japanese cuisine).
Karczma Polska, XII, Márvány utca 19, tel. 566–851, (Polish cuisine).
Kárpátia, V, Károlyi Mihály utca 4–8, tel. 173–596, until 11 p.m. (specialities from the Carpathian Mountains).
Napoletana, V, Petőfi tér, tel. 185–714, until midnight Mon. (Italian cuisine).
Öreghalász, IV, Árpád utca 20, tel. 694–192, until midnight (fish dishes).
Pepita Oroszlán, V, Váci utca 40, tel. 124–261 (Kosher cuisine).
Pest-Buda, I, Fortuna utca 3, tel. 569–849, until midnight (French cuisine).
Szecsuán, V, Roosevelt tér 5, tel. 172–502, until midnight (Chinese cuisine).
Szerb, V, Nagy Ignác utca 16, 111–858, until 10 p.m. (Serbian cuisine).
Szófia, V, Kossuth Lajos tér 13–15, tel. 118–232 , until 11 p.m. (Bulgarian cuisine).
Sirtos, VII, Csengery utca 24, tel. 410–772, until 11 p.m. (Greek cuisine).
Trofea, XIV, Erzsébet Irályné út 1, until 1 a.m. (game dishes).
Vörös Sárkány, VI, Népköztársaság útja 80, tel. 318–757, until 1 a.m. (Oriental cuisine).

Hungarian cuisine

Alföldi, V, Kecskeméti utca 4, tel. 174–404, until midnight.
Aranybárny, V, Harmincad utca 4, tel. 172–703, until midnight.
Fekete Holló Vendeglö 1, Orszagház utca 10, tel. 560–175.
Margitkert, II, Margit utca 15, tel. 354–791, until midnight.
Márványmenyasszony, I, Márvány utca 6, tel. 753–165, until midnight.
Mátyás Pince, V, Március 15 tér 7, tel. 181–650.
Megyeri Csárda, IV, Váci út 102, tel. 593–964, until midnight.
Ménes Csárda, V, Apáczai Csere J. utca 15, tel. 170–803, until 1 a.m.
Postakocsi, III, Fő tér 2, tel. 687–801, until 1 a.m.
Régi Országház, I, Országház utca 17, tel. 750–650, until 1 a.m.
Sipos, III, Fő tér 6, tel. 888–745, until midnight.
Szeged, XI, Bartók Béla út 1, tel. 666–503, until midnight.
Thököly, XIV, Thököly út 80, tel. 225–444, until midnight.
Trombitás, II, Retek utca 12, tel. 351–374, until 1 a.m.
Vadróza, II, Pentelei Moınar 12, tel. 351–118.
Vasmacska, III, Laktanya utca 3–5, tel. 887–123, until 2 a.m.

Wine bars

Aranyhordó, I, Tárnok utca 16, tel. 561–367, until midnight.
Borkatakomba, XXII, Nagytétenyi út 64, tel. 464–859, until midnight.
Fortuna Ház, I, Hess András tér 4, tel. 756–857.
Hirös, III, Külső Bécsi út 507, tel. 668–016.
La Bodega, XI, Tas vezér utca 9–11, tel. 612–250.
Nimród, V, Münnich Ferenc utca 24, tel. 116–098.
Vinceller, VII, Rákóczi út 90, 229–050.

Beer parlours

Bécsi, V, Eötvös Loránd utca 8, tel. 174–504.
Bowling, V, Szent Pál utca 1, tel. 186–316.

Fregatt, V, Molnár utca 26, tel. 189–997.
Kaltenberg I, IX, Kinizsí utca 30, tel. 189–792.
Prágaj Svejk, VII, Majakovskij utca 59, tel. 223–278.
Raabe-Diele, V, Szent István körút 13, tel. 316–533.
Vigadó, V. Vigadó. 1, tel, 181–598, until midnight.

See Cafés, Espressos, Tea Shops.   Coffee shops

Sailing (on Lake Balaton)

Sailing on Lake Balaton is very popular either in one's own boat
or in boats which can be hired on the lake (in Siófok, Balaton-
füred, Keszthely and other places).
For large yachts one needs the sail indicator "A". Visitors who
bring their own yachts to Hungary need a triptyque (carnet).
This triptyque can be obtained from the national Automobile
Clubs.
Since January 1976 motorboats have been banned from Lake
Balaton but sailing boats with auxiliary motors are allowed.
There are mooring-places for small boats on Lake Balaton in
the vicinity of the hotels and bungalow complexes. Larger
boats must tie up at Balatonfüred near the hotels Marina and
Annabella, in Tihany near the sailing club, in Balatonalmádi at
the sailing club and in Keszthely near the hotel Helikon boats'
slipway: very large boats in Balatonfüred, Siófok and in Tihany,
Keszthely.

Yacht Club WG, Pegasus Tours, H-1053 Budapest, Károlyi   Information for sailors
Mihály utca 5, tel. 171–444.

Ship/Boat Services

Surprising as it may sound, after Vienna Budapest, the capital
of the inland country of Hungary, is the most important of all
cruise destinations on Europe's second longest river. In recent
years the nearby Lake Balaton has become a very popular
sailing resort.

Danube

International Landing-stage (Danube Passenger Ships)   Landing-stages
V, Balgrád rakpart, tel: 181–953, 181–706 (international customs station, visas handed out).

Landing-stage for excursion ships and local services
V, Vigadó tér, tel: 181–223

From Budapest, landing-stage Vigadó tér, in the high season   Excursions
excursions are operated daily (at other times only at week-ends
and holidays) to Viségrad and Esztergom (see Danube Bend).

MAHART   Information
V, Apáczai Csere János utca 11, tel: 181–880
V, Vigadó tér, tel: 181–223
I, Bem József tér, tel: 354–907

See Getting to Budapest, by ship
See Travel Agents

Lake Balaton

Ferries

Between the peninsula of Tihany (north bank) and Szántód (south bank) there are frequent car and passenger ferries.

Excursions

During the high season excursions operate from all the important holiday centres. Small craft link all the larger places with a regular service.
Sometimes evening excursions with dancing and entertainment are available.

Information

See Travel Agents

Shopping

Although Budapest cannot be compared as a shopping centre with London, Munich, Milan or Paris, nevertheless the Hungarian capital offers the most comprehensive assortment of goods in eastern Europe. The main shopping streets are Váci utca, Kossuth Lajos utca, Rákóczi út, Múzeum körút, Tolbuhin körút, Kigjó utca and Népköztársaság útja, as well as the streets in the Castle district.

Sightseeing Programme

City Bus

There is a tour of the city by bus during the holiday season (details from IBUSZ, V, Felszabadulás tér).

Walkman Tourguide

For a small charge, the Budapest Tourist travel agency will hire you a Walkman Tourguide to a walk through the castle quarter.

Note

The following recommendations should provide the tourist who is visiting Budapest for the first time and does not have too much time with some ideas for getting the most out of his or her stay. Unless shown otherwise, the references in the text refer to the descriptions given in the "Budapest from A to Z" section of this book.

One day

For the traveller with only one day to spend in Budapest we would recommend an organised tour of the city by bus. During this excursion all the highlights of the Hungarian capital will be touched upon (see A to Z for details of most of the following landmarks): The old royal city of Buda, with its Castle Palace, Matthias Church and Fishermen's Bastion, the Gellért Hill with the Gellért Monument, Liberation Monument and Citadel, the Pest district with the imposing Parliament Building and beautiful Danube Corso, the Chain Bridge, the Inner Ring and the Outer Ring with the famous old Café Hungária, Heroes' Square with the Millennium Monument, not to mention the State

Opera, the City Woodland Park with the Castle Vajdahunyad, as well as Margaret Island with its famous Thermal Spa. After this exhausting tour of the city you can relax in one of numerous good cafés or espressos in the Castle Quarter or in the centre of Pest.

Anyone who wishes to get to know the city even better would be well advised to visit one of the world-famous spa establishments, especially typical of which is the historically venerated Gellért thermal bath in the hotel of the same name.

In the late afternoon a stroll through the Váci utca is a good idea. It is still Eastern Europe's most famous shopping street. Later you can enjoy the illuminations on Castle Hill and the Chain Bridge as seen from the Danube Corso. Finish off your evening with a visit to a restaurant offering typical Hungarian cuisine and gypsy music.

If you have two days to spend in Budapest then, using the above suggestions for a one-day visit as a basis, try to crystallise your impressions of the city still further. In the morning you could aim to visit the Parliament Building, the Castle Palace with its various museums and gallery, and the Matthias Church. In the afternoon take in Óbuda and the remains of the old Roman settlement at Aquincum. Also to be recommended are trips by cog-wheel railway to Széchenyi Hill (Széchenyi-hegy) or by chair-lift to John's Hill (János-hegy). An alternative choice would be a water-bus trip on the Danube, ending with a walk in the park and gardens on Margaret Island. Keep the evening free for a wine-tasting or a variety show.

Two days

In addition to seeing the most important sights, having three days at your disposal means you can go even further afield. An excursion by ship or coach to the entrancing countryside of the Danube Bend, north of Budapest will leave a lasting impression. Well worth seeing are the little medieval town of Szentendre, the hill-fortress of Visegrád and the old town of Esztergom, once the Hungarian royal residence, with its fine cathedral. A good alternative to an excursion to the Danube Bend would be a day's tour around Lake Balaton, where the Tihany Peninsula, Badacsony (well-known for its wine), the little town of Kesthely and the health resort of Héviz off to the west are all worth visiting.

Three days

See also Excursions

Souvenirs

In all tourist centres, souvenirs of various qualities are on offer. Highly original gifts, in addition to the Rubic Cube, are hand-made textiles (blouses, dresses, tablecloths, pillow-slips, etc.) which are quite often magnificently embroidered. Kalocsaer blouses, Matyó embroidery, jackets with felt decoration and woven rural articles are popular, as are Herend porcelain, Pecser china, pottery from Siebenburgen or carved wooden cutlery and vessels of the Puszta herdsmen tradition. Glassware, leather goods (especially elegant ladies' handbags), shoes, ties, belts and natural medicaments (pollen from blossoms, propolis, honey and medicinal herbs) are popular with tourists due to their relatively favourable prices.

Records made in Budapest studios of music by the famous Hungarian composers Bartók, Kodály, Goldmark and Liszt are always well worth buying, as are books and old prints which can often be found at reasonable prices in the local antiquarian shops.

The most sought after Budapest souvenirs are Hungarian salami, Barack (apricot brandy), Szilva (plum brandy), Tokay (dessert wine) and paprika and garlic of all kinds.

Spa Establishments (Gyógyfürdő)

Springs

The richest mineral springs in Europe are to be found in the area of the city of Budapest. 123 registered thermal springs service no less than 32 baths of which nine are officially recognised as spas. The most productive, which reach up to 76 °C (160 °F), arise along a geological fault which stretches from Gellért Hill (Gellért-hegy) northwards right out over Margaret Island.

Budapest

Dandárutcai

H-1095 Budapest, Dandár utca 5–7, tel. 137–084.
Treatment includes: thermal, steam and brine baths.
Opening times: Mon.–Fri. 7 a.m.–6 p.m., Sat. 7 a.m.–2 p.m., Sun. 6.30 a.m.–noon.

Gellért

H-1111 Budapest, Kelenhegyi út 4–6, tel. 666–166; situated in the XI district, at the west end of the Szabadság hid bridge.
Treatment includes: thermal, steam, wave, carbonic, brine and other baths, mud packs, physio- and electro-therapy, massage, sauna, solarium, etc.
Opening times: steam and normal baths Mon.–Fri. 6.30 a.m.–8 p.m., Sat. 6.30 a.m.–2 p.m., Sun. 6.30 a.m.–1 p.m.; wave baths and other treatments daily 6.30 a.m.–7 p.m.

Király

H-1021 Budapest, Fő utca 84, tel. 153–000.
Treatment includes: thermal, steam, brine and other baths, massage and sauna.
Opening times: men only Mon. Wed. and Fri. 6.30 a.m.–7 p.m.; ladies only Tues. and Thur. 6.30 a.m.–7 p.m., Sat. 6.30 a.m.–2 p.m.

Lukács

H-1023 Budapest, Frankel Léo út 25, tel. 154–280.
Treatment includes: thermal, steam, mud, brine, carbonated wave and other baths, massage, gymnastics, physio- and electro-therapy, drinking fountain.
Opening times: steam baths Mon.–Fri. 6.30 a.m.–7 p.m., Sat. 6.30 a.m.–2 p.m., Sun. 6.30 a.m.–1 p.m.; mud and sunken baths Mon.–Fri. 6.30 a.m.–7 p.m., Sat. 6.30 a.m.–2 p.m.; wave bath Mon.–Sat. 6 a.m.–8 p.m., Sun. 6 a.m.–5 p.m.; drinking fountain Mon.–Sat. 6 a.m.–7 p.m., Sun. 6 a.m.–noon.

Pesterzsébet

H-1203 Budapest, Vizisport út 2, tel. 478–581.
Treatment includes: thermal and steam baths, massage.
Opening times: ladies only Mon., Wed., Fri. 7 a.m.–6 p.m.; men only Tues., Thur., Sat. 7 a.m.–6 p.m.

H-1013 Budapest, Hadnagy utca 8, tel. 758–373   Rác
Treatment includes: thermal and other baths, massage, solar-
ium, conditioning.
Opening times: Mon.–Sat. 6.30 a.m.–7 p.m.

H-1113 Budapest, Döbrentei tér 9, tel. 754–449.   Rudas
Treatment includes: thermal, steam, wave and other baths,
massage, physio- and electro-therapy, drinking fountain.
Opening times: N.B. Men only! Steam bath Mon.–Fri. 6 a.m.–
7 p.m., Sat. 6 a.m.–1 p.m., Sun. 6 a.m.–noon; wave bath Mon.–
Fri. 6 a.m.–6 p.m., Sat. 6 a.m.–8 p.m., Sun. 6 a.m.–noon; drinking fountain Mon.–Sat. 6 a.m.–7 p.m.

H-1146 Budapest, Állatkerti körút 11, tel. 210–310.   Széchenyi
Treatment includes: thermal, steam, brine, wave and other
baths, mud-packs, massage, gymnastics, physio- and electro-
therapy, solarium, sauna, drinking fountain.
Opening times: thermal basin and baths Mon.–Fri. 6.30 a.m.–
7 p.m., Sat. 6.30 a.m.–1 p.m., Sun. 6.30 a.m.–noon; swimming
bath daily 6 a.m.–6 p.m.; sauna Mon.–Sat. 6 a.m.–6 p.m.; drinking fountain daily 7 a.m.–6.30 p.m.

H-1042 Budapest, Árpád út 114, tel. 690–344.   Újpesti
Treatment includes: thermal and steam baths and massage.
Opening times: Mon.–Fri. 6.30 a.m.–6 p.m., Sat. 6.30 a.m.–
1 p.m., Sun. 6.30 a.m.–noon.

Margitsziget (Margaret Island), tel. 111–000.   Hotel Thermál
Treatment includes: thermal and other baths, massage, mud-
packs, physio- and electro-therapy, gymnastics, irrigation,
sauna.
Opening times: daily 7 a.m.–9 p.m.

Lake Balaton and district

North bank of Lake Balaton.   Balatonfüred
Treatment includes: carbonic and sulphur baths, mud packs,
massage.
Opening times: Mon.–Fri. 7 a.m.–2 p.m.

5 km north-west of Kesthely (west end of Lake Balaton).   Héviz
Treatment includes: remedial bathing (water slightly radioactive and sulphurous), remedial mud packs, weight-loss bathing, massage, gymnastics, electro-therapy.
Opening times: daily 8 a.m.–5 p.m.

Sport

Népstadion   Stadiums
XIV, Istvánmezei út 1–3

Kisstadion
Szabó József utca 1
nearby is the Millenáris Sportsground (Millenáris sportpálya)

Sport

New "Budapest" sports hall

Horse-racing tracks	Budapest Riding Club Kerepesi út 7, tel. 131–349
	Ady-liget Riding Club Feketefej utca, tel. 164–267
	Trotting race-track (Ügető-pálya) VIII, Kerepesi út 9
	Racetrack (Lóverseny tér galopp-pálya) X, Dobi István utca 2
Tennis-courts	Dózsa teniszstadion XIII, Margaret Island
	Varosmajor teniszstadion II, Varosmajor
Sports hall	Sportcsarnok Nemzeti (National Sports Hall) XIV, Istvánmezei út
	"Budapest" Sportcsarnok (Sports Hall "Budapest") XIV, Hungária körút
	Olimpiai Csarnok (Olympia Sports Hall) XIV, Verseny utca

Körcsarnok
(Circular Sports Hall)
XIV, Verseny utca

Játék Csarnok
(Jatek Sports Hall)
XIV, near the Népstadion

Millenáris kerékpár-pálya   Cycle racetrack
XIV, Szabó József utca

Műjegpálya   Artificial ice-rink
XIV, Városliget

Gellért   Open all year covered and
XI, Kelenhegyi út 4   open-air swimming-pools

Hajós Alfréd sportuszoda
XIII, Margaret Island

Komjádi Béla sportuszoda
II, Komjádi Béla utca 2–4

Csillahegyi
III, Pusztakúti utca 3

Lukács
II, Frankel Leó utca 25–29

Szabadság
XIII, Népfürdő utca 30

Széchenyi
XIV, Állatkerti körút 11

Ujpesti
IV, Árpád út 114–120

Cinkotai   Open May–Sept.
XVI, Allomás tér 1   open-air swimming-pools

Csepeli
XXI, Hollandi út

Albertfalvai
XI, Szabadság út 84

Kispesti
XIX, Ady Endre út 99

Pesterzsébet
XX, Csepeli átjáró

Pestlőrinc
XVIII, Vörös Hadsereg útja 180

Taxis

Palatinus
XIII, Margaret Island

Rákoscsabai
XVII, Kelecsényi út

Római
III, Lópormalom dűlő

Spas   See entry

Winter sports   Ski-lift János-hegy
                            Natural ice-rinks in Városliget

Taxis

Fötaxi   Tel. 222–222

Volántaxi   Tel. 666–666

Buda-Taxi   Tel. 294–000, 166–459

City-Taxi   Tel. 228–855

Rádio-Taxi   Tel. 271–271

Taxiunió   Tel. 555–000

Car Rental   See entry

Telegrams

See Post
See Telephone

Telephone

Local calls   A local call (from 7 a.m. to 6 p.m. 3 minutes; from 6 p.m. to
                            7 a.m. 6 minutes) costs 1.5 forints (from coin operated boxes
                            a 2-forint coin)

Dialled calls   Calls can be dialled directly in Budapest including calls made
                            from many coin-operated boxes (minimum 10 forints; follow
                            the instructions carefully).

International dialling codes Great Britain: 0044
                            United States and Canada: 001

tel: 172–200   Information for long-
                                                               distance calls in English and
                                                               other foreign languages

tel: 09   Telephone exchange for
                                                               international calls

Annexe of Main Post Office   Long-distance call office
V, Petőfi Sándor utca 17–19
Opening times: Mon.–Sat. 7 a.m.–9 p.m., Sun. and holidays
8 a.m.–1 p.m.

tel: 02   Telegrams

See entry   Post

Theatres

Arena Theatre (Körszínhaz)   Addresses
XIV, Városliget, tel: 224–251

Atila-József Theatre (József Attila Színház)
XIII, Váci út 63, tel: 208–238

Castle Theatre (Várszínház)
I, Szinház utca 1–3, tel: 868–664

Civic Operetta Theatre
Fővárosi Operett Szinház)
VI, Nagymező utca 17, tel: 126–470

Congress Centre (Kongresszusi kožpont)
XII, Jagelló út

Corona Podium (Korona Pódium; literary readings)
I, Dísz tér 16

Erkel Theatre (Erkel Színház)
VIII, Köztarsaság tér 30, tel: 330–540

Josephtown Theatre (Józsefvárosi Színház)
VIII, Kulich Gyula tér 6, tel: 338–620

József-Katona Theatre (Katona József Színház)
V, Petőfi Sándor utca 6, tel: 186–559

Literary Theatre Miklós Radnóti
(Radnóti Miklós Irodalmi Színpad)
VI, Nagymező utca 11, tel: 420–561

Madách Studio Theatre (Madách-Kamaraszínház)
VII, Madách tér 6, tel: 226–422

Madách Theatre (Madách Színház)
VII, Lenin körút 29–33, tel: 220–677

Microscope Theatre (Mikroszkóp színpad)
VI, Nagymező utca 22–24, tel: 113–322

Theatres

National Theatre (Nemzéti színház)
VII, Hevesi Sándor tér 2, tel: 413–849

Odry Theatre (Odry színpad)
VIII, Vas utca 2, tel: 337–503

Old Theatre (Játékszin)
VI, Lenin körút 106, tel: 121–430

Opera House (Magyar Allami Operaház)
VI, Népköztarsaság útja 22, tel: 320–126

Pest Theatre (Pesti Színház)
V, Váci utca 9, tel: 185–547

Puppet Theatre (Allami Bábszinház)
VI, Népköztarsaság útja 69,
tel: 422–702
and also at
VI, Jókai tér 10, tel: 120–622

Thalia Theatre (Thalia Színház)
VI, Nagymező utca 22–24, tel: 310–500

Theatre of Comedy (Vigszínház)
XIII, Szent István körút 14, tel: 110–430

University Theatre (Egyetemi Színpad)
V, Pesti Barnabás utca 1, tel: 183–311

Variety Theatre (Vidám Színpad)
VI, Révay utca 18, tel: 311–311

Open-air theatres

Buda Park Theatre (Budai Parkszínpad)
XI, Kosztolányi Dezső tér, tel: 669–849

Open-air theatre on Margaret Island (Margitszigeti Szabadteri Színpad)
XIII, Margitsziget (Margaret Island), tel: 112–463

Dominican Courtyard of the Hilton Hotel
I, Hess András tér 1–3

Open-air theatre in Városmajor Park (Városmajori Szabadteri Színpad)
XII, Városmajori Park, tel: 353–178

Advance booking

Theatre box offices are normally open on Thur.–Sat. 3–5 p.m. The following advance booking offices are open during normal business hours:
VI, Népköztarsaság útja 18, tel: 120–100
II, Moszkva tér 3, tel: 359–136
V, Vörösmarty tér 1, tel: 176–222

Advance programme information

Tourinform, tel: 179–800
Mon.–Fri. 7 a.m.–9 p.m., Sat. 7 a.m.–8 p.m., Sun. 8 a.m.–1 p.m.

Most performances begin at 8.30 p.m.

Commencement of performances

See entry

Newspapers

Time

Hungary observes Central European Time (Greenwich Mean Time + 1 hour); in summer Central European Summer Time (Daylight Saving) (Greenwich Mean Time + 2 hours).

Tipping

As Hungary has got nearer and nearer to Western standards in recent years, so the concept of giving tips has also gained ground. Whereas the service charge was usually included in the bill, today restaurant staff, taxi drivers and hairdressers expect a 10–15% tip. A petrol pump attendant expects at least 10 forints for his services.

General remarks

Gipsy bands often play in public-houses and then pass the hat round.

Gipsy bands

Tourist Information

The most important addresses for information concerning a proposed tour of Budapest are the IBUSZ Bureaux:

Hungarian State Travel Bureaux IBUSZ

Danube Travel Limited, Central Agent IBUSZ Hungary, 6 Conduit Street, London W1R 9TG, tel: (071) 493 0263.

Great Britain

IBUSZ Hungarian Travel Ltd, Suite 520, 630 Fifth Avenue, Rockefeller Center, New York, NY 10020, tel: (212) 582 7412; toll free 800/367–7878.

United States

Tourinform, Süto utca 2 (Pest district, near Deák tér, open daily 8 a.m.–8 p.m.), tel: 179–800.

Budapest

IBUSZ, H-1364 Budapest V, Felszabadulás tér 5, tel: 186–866.

Budapest Tourist, H-1051 Budapest V, Roosevelt tér 5, tel: 173–555.

See entry

Travel agents

Traffic Regulations

Vehicle documents	International driving permit is not obligatory but a national driving licence and registration document should be taken.
Nationality plate	Vehicles must display an oval nationality plate.
Vehicle insurance	In Hungary accidents must be reported if possible within 24 hours, but at the latest on the next working day to the relevant authority which, in Budapest, is the Department of International Motor Insurance of the State Insurance Company (AB, Budapest XI, Hamzsabégi út 60, tel: 669–755); elsewhere in Hungary it is the branch offices of the State Insurance Company.
Seat belts	The wearing of seat belts in the front seats is compulsory.
Children	Children under six years of age may not travel in front seats.
Alcohol ban	In Hungary it is an offence to drive after drinking any alcohol.
	Vehicles travel on the right.
Speed limits	In built-up areas: cars 60 km/h (37 mph), buses, cars with trailers and motor cycles 50 km/h (31 mph). On main roads: cars 80 km/h (50 mph), cars with trailers and motor cycles 70 km/h (43 mph). On motorways: cars 100 km/h (62 mph), cars with trailers and motor cycles 80 km/h (50 mph).
Special rules for motor cyclists	Motor cyclists must wear a helmet at all times. They must also used dipped headlights during the day.
Filling stations (Gas stations)	Near frontier points and on the principal roads these can be found every 20 to 50 km. Petrol can be obtained without coupons (Super 92 octane and Extra 98 octane). Diesel fuel can only be obtained with coupons which can be bought at frontier points. There is no repayment for coupons which may remain when the driver leaves Hungary.
Lead-free petrol	Along the principal roads leading out of Austria, in Budapest and around Lake Balaton there are now quite a number of petrol stations where you can get lead-free petrol.
Road tolls	There are plans afoot to charge tolls on Hungarian motorways.
Breakdown assistance	See entry

Travel Agents

Selection	Budapest Tourist V, Roosevelt tér 5, H-1051 Budapest (Pest), tel: 173–555 Szentháromság utca 5 (Castle Quarter), tel: 736–372

IBUSZ
Petőfi tér 3, H-1052 Budapest (Pest: open day and night),
tel: 185–707.
Felszabadulás tér 5, H-1053 Budapest (Pest), tel: 186–866
Tanács körút 31c, H-1075 Budapest, tel: 423–140

Blaguss Volanbusz
Engels tér 5 (Building B), H-1051 Budapest (Pest), tel: 177–777

Express
Semmelweiss utca 4, H-1052 Budapest (Pest), tel: 176–634

Malev Airtours
Roosevelt tér 2, H-1051 Budapest, tel: 181–918

Travel Documents

For entry to Hungary a valid passport is necessary. Citizens of non-socialist countries and stateless persons can only enter Hungary with a visa. Visas are obtainable, normally within 48 hours, from all Hungarian consulates abroad. A visa can also be obtained at a road frontier crossing point, at the airport and at the international shipping office in Budapest.
Members of travel groups (spending four days or less in Hungary) who enter the country from Austria do not require a visa. Foreigners with a visa can remain up to the time stated on it (normally 30 days). A transit visa is valid for 48 hours.

Passport and visa

Citizens of non-socialist countries must register within 24 hours of arrival or if they change their address in Hungary. Hotels, camp sites and accommodation offices will register for visitors and confirm this on the official document which is inspected by the Hungarian frontier police on departure from the country. Foreigners who stay in private houses must register personally: in Budapest at the police station of the district in which they are staying, elsewhere at the appropriate regional, area or urban police station, the head of the family can register for everyone.

Registration with police

The visitor's permit can be extended 48 hours before time of expiry at the place of registration, at district police offices or at the relevant department of the Budapest police headquarters (VI, Népköztársaság útja 12). Loss of a passport, travel documents, visitor's permit or exit document must be notified immediately to the nearest police station. On the strength of the certificate issued new travel documents must be obtained from the appropriate consulate within three days, for which the relevant office of the Hungarian Ministry of the Interior (KEOKH, Budapest VI, Rudas László utca 45) will issue an exit permit.

Extension of visitor's permit

Anyone violating the registration regulations or exceeding the period stated on the visitor's permit is liable to a fine of up to 3,000 forints.

Violation of registration regulations

See: Currency Regulations
      Customs Regulations
      Frontier Crossing Points
      Traffic Regulations

When to go

Note

The best time to go to Hungary is between April and October, spring and autumn being particularly delightful. In summer it can be very dry and hot; the water temperature in Lake Balaton then usually climbs above 23°C (73°F).

In the colder period of the year, from October onwards, Budapest is much quieter. A few tourists come only at Christmas and the New Year. It should be borne in mind that the Hungarian winter can be bitterly cold.

Climatic table

Month	Temperatures in °C(°F) Av. max.	Av. min.	Sunshine hours per day	Days with rain	Rainfall amounts in mm(ins)
January	1.2(34.2)	−4.0(24.8)	1.9	13	37(1.5)
February	4.1(39.4)	−2.3(27.9)	3.0	12	44(1.7)
March	10.2(50.4)	1.5(34.7)	4.4	11	38(1.5)
April	16.8(62.2)	6.6(43.9)	6.2	11	45(1.8)
May	21.9(71.4)	11.3(52.3)	8.1	13	72(2.8)
June	25.5(78.0)	14.7(58.5)	9.0	13	69(2.7)
July	27.7(81.9)	16.4(61.5)	9.6	10	56(2.2)
August	27.3(81.1)	15.7(60.3)	8.7	9	47(1.9)
September	23.2(73.8)	11.9(53.4)	6.5	7	33(1.3)
October	15.9(60.6)	6.9(44.4)	4.3	10	57(2.2)
November	8.1(46.6)	−3.1(26.4)	2.2	14	70(2.8)
December	3.6(38.5)	−1.0(30.2)	1.3	13	46(1.8)
Year	15.5(59.9)	6.7(44.1)	5.6	136	614(24.2)

Youth hostels

Information

Express Travel Agency
Semmelweiss utca 4, H-1052 Budapest (Pest), tel: 176–634, open Mon.–Sat. 8 a.m.–6 p.m.
Information kiosk on the Eastern Railway Station (Keleti pályaudvar).

Useful Telephone Numbers

	Telephone
Emergency calls	
– First-Aid/Rescue Service	04
– Police	07
– Fire Brigade	05
– Breakdown Assistance	691–831, 693–714
Information	
– Tourist Information TOURINFORM	179–800
– National Railways	429–150
– International Railways	224–052
– Long Distance Buses	172–562
– Air Travel	572–122
Foreign Office KEOKH	180–800
Automobile Club	
– Autóklub	260–668
Embassies and Consulates	
– Great Britain	182–888
– USA	126–450
– Canada	767–686
Air Lines	
– British Airways	183–299
– Pan Am	187–922
– Malév	189–033
Lost Property Offices	
– Central Lost Property Office	174–961
– Budapest Transport (BKV)	226–613
Taxi	222–222, 666–666, etc.
Telephone	
– Long-distance Calls (foreign languages)	172–200
– International Exchange	09
– Dialling Codes:	
To Great Britain	0044
To America and Canada	001

Plans of the Budapest Underground (Metro)